From Your Friends At **The MAILBOX®**

YO-DAB-748

Teacher Tips
Grades 1-3

Editor In Chief
Marge Michel

Product Director
Kathy Wolf

Editors
Susan M. Hohbach, Cynthia Holcomb, Sharon Murphy

Copy Editors
Lynn Bemer Coble, Carol Rawleigh, Jennifer Rudisill
Debbie Shoffner, Gina Sutphin

Artists
Jennifer Tipton Bennett, Cathy Spangler Bruce
Clevell Harris, Susan Hodnett, Donna K. Teal

Typographers
Scott Lyons, Lynette Maxwell

Cover Artist
Jennifer Tipton Bennett

Teacher Tips
Grades 1-3

About This Book

We've compiled hundreds of never-before-published ideas sent from our subscribers to *The Mailbox®* magazine—The Idea Magazine For Teachers™. These ideas were sent to The Education Center, Inc., from elementary teachers from all over the United States and Canada.

The ideas in this resource book are arranged so that you can refer to a topic quickly and choose just the idea you need. In each section, you'll find creative ways to teach a skill, management tips, or activities to fill in a few extra minutes of the teaching day. Most of the ideas are adaptable to any primary grade level. Look in several sections for ideas to suit your individual needs.

Just turn these pages to find timesaving, teacher-tested tips to help make your teaching easier and more creative!

Table Of Contents

A Class Of Green Thumbs

With this green-thumb idea, your students won't be the only ones growing during the school year. At the beginning of each year, purchase an easy-to-care-for plant, such as a philodendron, to keep in the center of each table or group of desks. Put the students at each table in charge of caring for their table's plant. Invite each group of students to name their plant, decorate it during the holidays, and measure its growth throughout the year. You'll notice that as the plants grow, so does your students' sense of responsibility. By the end of the year, healthy plants and responsible children will abound in your classroom!

Sarah Mertz—Grs. 1–2
Owenton, KY

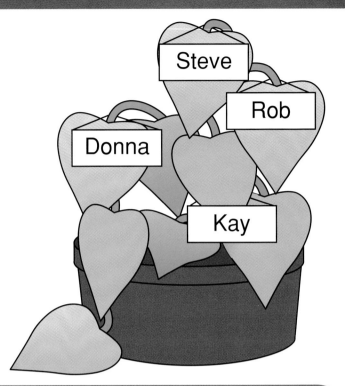

ABC Supply List

Looking for a unique way to ask parents for classroom supplies? Try this idea that will have parents sending in their extra ABCs—Any Beautiful Collectibles for the classroom! Duplicate a copy of the supply list on page 145 and reprogram, if necessary, to fit the supply needs of your classroom. Send home a copy of your personalized supply list with each child. Parents will enjoy the opportunity to supply materials for the classroom as well as participate in a creative scavenger hunt with their children.

Michelle Marconi—Gr. 1
James K. Polk Elementary
Alexandria, VA

Portrait Time

Break the ice on the first day of school with this drawing activity. Ask each student to draw a picture of you and guess some of your "favorites," such as color, food, and hobby. After students have completed their portraits of you, share with them your "favorites." Then invite each child to draw a picture of himself and share his "favorites." Your youngsters will be delighted at this chance to get to know their classmates and especially you!

Name And Toss

Help students learn their classmates' names with this "getting acquainted" activity. Set the stage for the activity by having students introduce themselves to the class. Have students stand in a large circle formation; then hand a beach ball to one player. To begin play, the player holding the ball calls out the name of a classmate and gently tosses the ball to that student. The student who receives the ball names a different classmate and tosses the ball to that student. Play continues until each student has had a chance to name and toss. Your youngsters will have a ball learning their classmates' names.

Cindy Ward—Grs. 1–4
Learning Disabilities Teacher
Yellow Branch Elementary
Rustburg, VA

First-Day Puzzle

Welcome your students on the first day of school with personalized puzzles. In advance, purchase a class supply of precut puzzles. Use permanent markers to personalize each puzzle and add some artwork. Take each puzzle apart and place the pieces in an envelope or plastic bag. Then write each child's name on the outside of her envelope or bag.

On the first day of school, place each child's puzzle on her desk. As students enter the classroom they'll be thrilled to see the puzzles at their seats. Students will enjoy putting the puzzles together to see their names and you'll be free to greet new arrivals at the door. Children can take the puzzles home at the end of the day for a keepsake of their first day in your classroom.

Arlene G. Phillippy—Gr. 3
Hershey Elementary School
Hershey, PA

Welcoming Wreath

Add some pizzazz to your classroom's door with this easy-to-make welcome wreath. Purchase a grapevine wreath from a craft store. Use hot glue to attach crayons, a small bottle of glue, a pencil, a small plastic apple, and various other school-related items to the wreath. Add a bow made from two yards of a school-theme ribbon to the bottom of the wreath. As a final touch, use a permanent black marker to write your name and room number on one or two of the items. Then suspend the wreath on a nail hammered in your door. Students, parents, and colleagues are all sure to notice this one-of-a-kind wreath.

Amy Ruff—Gr. 2
Inman Elementary
Inman, SC

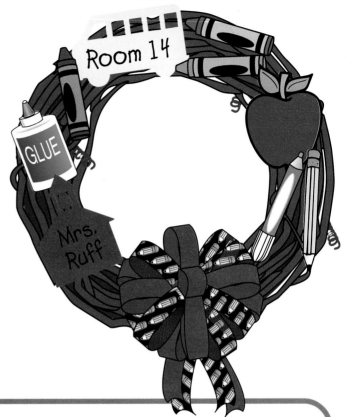

Easy First-Day Dismissal

Looking for a way to eliminate first-day dismissal dilemmas? Then try this tip! Make a nametag for each student that coordinates with his mode of transportation from school. For example, carpoolers will all have a specific color of nametag, walkers will have another color of nametag, and each set of bus riders will have a different color of nametag. When it's time for dismissal, group students according to the color of their nametags. You will easily be able to see how each student will be getting home—therefore, no more hectic dismissals!

Peggy Williams—Gr. 2, South Columbia Elementary, Martinez, GA

Signature Lotto

Help students learn the names of their classmates with this personalized activity. Duplicate a class supply of blank grids containing as many boxes as you have students. Have students collect their classmates' signatures in all the blank boxes. Then call students' names at random and have children mark their grids. The first student who completes a row in any direction is the winner. For an added twist, provide grids with an extra box so students can collect your signature too. Students are sure to have a whole "lotto" fun with this activity!

Please Sign!

Try using this twist on the usual autograph book as a "getting acquainted" activity. In advance staple five pieces of unlined paper between two construction-paper covers for each child. Ask each student to decorate his front cover. Next have him label the first page in his book "My Classmates" and then make a list of numbers down the left side of his book (one number per student in the class). Then have him label each of the following four pages with a different question such as "What is your favorite book?" or "How many brothers and sisters do you have?"

To fill in his book, the student asks a classmate to sign his book. The classmate chooses a number on the first page and signs her name beside it. She answers the questions on the next four pages by writing her number and the answer beside it on each page. Once each child's book has been signed by all of his classmates, ask students to refer to their books to answer questions such as "Who in the class is an only child?" or "Who said their favorite book was *The True Story Of The Three Little Pigs?*" It won't take long before your students feel like old friends!

Amy Flanigan—Substitute Teacher
Garrett County School System
Mt. Lake Park, MD

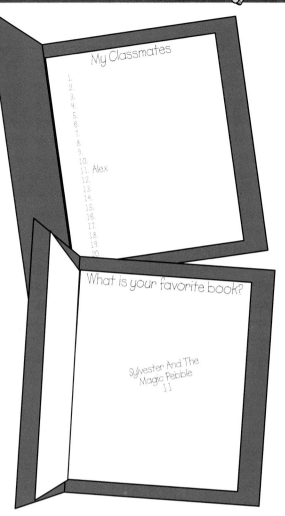

Sculpt Away The Jitters!

Help students get over the first-day jitters with this activity. Before students enter the classroom on the first day of school, place a ball of store-bought or homemade play dough on each student's desk. Invite students to mold the play dough at their desks as you greet new arrivals. Students will be so busy creating, they'll forget all about any jitters they might have had. Then at the end of the day, give each child a plastic bag to take his play dough home as a gift from you. Students will remember their first day in your classroom as a positive experience!

Jeannie Hinyard—Gr. 2
Welder Elementary School
Sinton, TX

Classroom Scavenger Hunt

To make sure students are aware of the locations of various classroom items, send students on a classroom scavenger hunt. Prepare a list to include items such as the pencil sharpener, extra paper, the mailboxes, the trash can, and other frequently used classroom items. Duplicate and distribute a copy of the list to each child. Instruct the student to check off each item on his list as he finds it in the classroom. For an added challenge, give students a time limit of approximately five minutes. After the scavenger hunt is complete, ask for volunteers to show the class where each item is found in the classroom. In no time at all, your youngsters will be familiarized with their classroom.

Beth Fondale—Gr. 2
St. Rose School
Junction City, OH

Name_____ Claire Reynolds

Classroom Scavenger Hunt

Please find:
- ☑ 1. pencil sharpener
- ☐ 2. trash can
- ☐ 3. extra paper
- ☐ 4. the mailboxes

Cindy Chris
Tracy

Pick A Stick

Do your students need a little extra help learning their classmates' names? Then try this idea! Write each child's name on one end of an individual craft stick; then place all the sticks, name end down, in a decorated can. Have students sit in a circle. Ask one student to pick a stick from the can. That student must read the name on the stick, give the stick to you, and then take the can to the student whose name he chose. Play continues until all the sticks are out of the can. Each student will eagerly await his turn to pick a stick and find his classmate.

Cindy Ward—Grs. 1–4
Learning Disabilities Teacher
Yellow Branch Elementary
Rustburg, VA

A Royal Welcome

Roll out the red carpet to welcome your students back to school. Cut a wide strip of red bulletin-board paper to fit in the entrance of your classroom. Label the paper with "Welcome" and each student's name. If desired, cover the paper with clear Con-Tact® paper to keep it from tearing. Then tape the edges of the paper to the floor. Look for smiling faces as your students enter each morning!

Places To Go!

Busy, busy, busy! Places to go and things to learn—all in one school year. Set the stage for a fun-filled year by reading aloud *Oh, The Places You'll Go* by Dr. Seuss. Invite your students to share what they expect to learn this year. Record their responses on a piece of chart paper. Then add to the chart other things that your students will be learning throughout the school year. Label the chart "Goals for [school year];" then display the chart on a classroom wall. After a goal has been reached, invite a student to place a check beside it on the chart. At the end of the year, use this chart to remind your students of all the places they have been!

Susan Johnson—Gr. 3, Steiner Ranch Elementary, Austin, TX

Decorate With Names

Use your youngsters' names for colorful decorations around the room! Use a die-cut machine and bright colors of construction paper to make several cutout shapes of each letter in the alphabet. Provide each child with the letters necessary to spell his name. Then instruct him to glue the edges of the letters together as shown. Use a length of yarn to suspend each name from the ceiling. What a decoration— bright, easy-to-make, and personalized!

Deborah Ross—Primary Teacher
Wayland Alexander School
Hartford, KY

Picture-Perfect Alphabet

Use your students' smiling faces to make a class book. Take a photograph of all students whose names begin with the letter *A*. Label the photo with a capital and a lowercase *a*. Continue to group students alphabetically, taking a picture for each letter represented. Label an 8 1/2" x 11" piece of light-colored construction paper for each letter in the alphabet. Glue each photograph on its page; then have each child sign her name on the page with her picture. Add a construction-paper cover and assemble the photograph pages alphabetically into a class book titled "Picture-Perfect Alphabet." Not only does this activity help students learn their classmates' names, but it provides an easy-to-make, personalized addition to your classroom.

Lights! Camera! Action!

Create a video to show at Open House featuring your favorite stars—your students! To begin the tape, record a student offering a greeting at the door to welcome viewers into the classroom. Tape a brief tour of the classroom; then have each student introduce himself. Next capture footage of normal classroom activities and routines. To conclude the recording, arrange for a co-worker to tape you being interviewed by a student. Parents will appreciate this chance to have an inside look at their youngsters' daily activities. The tape is also ideal to send home for parents who were unable to attend Open House. Be prepared for rave reviews—and maybe even a few requests for copies!

Laura Reeder—Gr. 2
Sara Collins Elementary
Greenville, SC

On The Road To Success

Need a nifty way to show parents and students the thematic units that will be covered throughout the school year? Try writing the units on a road-map outline as shown. Be sure to include vacations and holidays. Once the yearly plan is complete, duplicate one copy to display in the classroom and one copy to give to each parent at Open House. Each time you conclude a thematic unit, invite a child to color that section of the road. At a glance parents and students will be able to see what fun things lie on the road ahead!

Vicki Casso—Gr. 1
Laveen Elementary School
Laveen, AZ

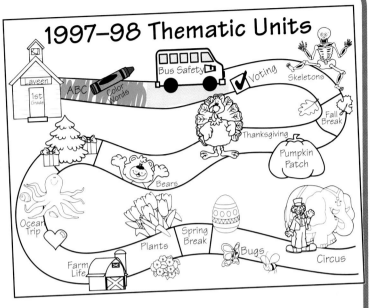

Open House Silhouette Hunt

Turn parents into detectives with this unique tip for an Open House hunt. Use an overhead projector to create each child's silhouette on black paper. Cut out and mount these on colored paper. On another piece of paper, have each child write five clues about herself. Mount each child's set of clues beside her silhouette. Have each child write her name on the back of her paper. Display each child's likeness on a classroom wall.

As parents enter the classroom at Open House, invite them to hunt for their own child's silhouette. This activity can be used to keep parents busy while you wait for others to arrive. Or it can serve as a great warm-up activity! Either way parents will have fun as they hunt for their special youngsters!

Janice Manson—Gr. 2
Bellaire Elementary School
Killeen, TX

A Warm Welcome

Parents' first impression of Open House will be a positive one with this unique idea. Instruct each child to trace his hand on a piece of colored construction paper. Have him cut out the resulting shape and write his name on it. Label a piece of poster board with "Welcome"; then glue each student's hand-shaped cutout around the greeting. On the evening of Open House, display the sign outside your door. Parents can't help but start their evening off with smiles when they see the children's warm welcome!

Dear Sam,
  Daddy and I loved looking at all your work. Your desk was so nice and clean. We are very proud of you.

  Hugs and kisses,
  Mom & Dad

Notes From The Folks

So your students' parents think they're too old for schoolwork? Not so! Add a twist to this year's Open House by giving parents a writing assignment. Place a sheet of paper and a pencil on each student's desk before parents arrive. Ask each parent to take a few minutes to write a note to his or her child and place it in his desk. Encourage parents to comment on how proud they are of their children. If there are some children whose parents were unable to attend, jot quick messages to them, too, so that everyone will get a cheerful note in the morning. Imagine the smiles you'll see on your youngsters' faces when they find a note from their parents tucked in their desks.

Ann Margaret Eddy—Gr. 2
Royal Oaks Christian School
Arroyo Grande, CA

Whoo Am I?

Parents will be all the wiser about their children after this Open House activity. Supply each child with a copy of the owl pattern on page 146. Encourage each student to color and cut out his owl, then write three clues about himself on the outside stomach area. Next have each student fold his owl on the dotted line and sign his name on the inside of the owl cutout. Mount the owls on a classroom wall so that students' names cannot be seen unless the cutouts are opened. Challenge parents to try to find their own child's owl. Everyone will get a hoot out of this entertaining activity!

Beth Fondale—Gr. 2
St. Rose School
Junction City, OH

1. I am a boy.
2. I have 1 brother and 1 sister.
3. My dog's name is Buddy.

Family Pack

Do you find yourself with too much to say at Open House and not enough time to say it? If so, make this parent-friendly booklet. Begin by creating a decorative cover that includes your name, grade level, room number, school year, and the title "Family Pack." On the next page write a short summary of your background and teaching style. Then include pages detailing the class schedule, class rules, supplies needed, homework policy, and importance of parent volunteers. Duplicate a class supply of each page and compile into booklets to give to parents at Open House. Parents will appreciate the family packs full of answers to frequently asked beginning-of-the-year questions.

Daniel Kuball
Trinity First School
Minneapolis, MN

Family Pack 1997–1998

Mr. Kuball
2nd grade
Room 22

The Birthday Bag

Spread some birthday cheer on each student's special day with gifts galore from the birthday bag! At the beginning of the school year, decorate a bag with a birthday theme and fill it with a class supply of birthday pencils, certificates of well-wishes, birthday nametags, and an assortment of birthday stickers. When a student's birthday arrives, call him to your desk, reach into the bag, and present him with an assortment of goodies. By collecting a class supply at the beginning of the year, you'll be prepared to brighten the day when each birthday rolls around.

Peggy Seibel—Gr. 2
St. Mary's School
Ellis, KS

Photo Finish

Celebrate each student's birthday with a lasting memory—a photograph! Greet the birthday child by the classroom calendar, making sure to mark the special day. Have a Polaroid® photo taken of the two of you in front of the calendar, then write a birthday message across the bottom of the picture. Present the photo to the student as a keepsake of the big day. Say, "cheese!"

Julie Furleigh—Gr. 2, La Salle Avenue School, Los Angeles, CA

A Sharp Idea!

For an inexpensive way to have your students make a gift for the birthday child, provide a new, unsharpened yellow pencil and a supply of fine-tipped permanent markers in assorted colors. Encourage each student to draw a design on the pencil. Present it to the birthday child at the beginning of the day, and he'll be proud to use the gift on all of his assignments. What a practical way to say, "Happy birthday!"

Rita Petrocco
Nepean, Ontario
Canada

Birthday Booklet

Celebrate each student birthday with a booklet of best wishes. For each day of honor, prepare or purchase a booklet of blank pages. Decorate the cover with drawings or stickers that reflect the birthday theme. Autograph one page of the booklet and include a cheery greeting or drawing; then have each student write a message and sign his name to one page of the booklet. Present the completed booklet to the birthday child as a remembrance of his special day. Happy, happy, day!

Peggy Morin—Gr. 2
Miller School
Wilton, CT

Super Celebration

Students will enjoy being the guests of honor at a special celebration in recognition of their birthdays. Set aside one day each month for a special luncheon to honor students who have birthdays during that month. Invite the birthday students to dine in the classroom with you instead of eating in the cafeteria that day. Create a special atmosphere by having placemats on the desks or by having a floral centerpiece at a table. Provide a cupcake topped with a candle for each birthday student. Complete the meal with a chorus of "Happy Birthday To You" as each student makes a wish and blows out his candle.

Leigh Anne Newsom
E. W. Chittum Elementary
Chesapeake, VA

The Birthday Corner

Dedicate a special corner of your room to student birthdays. Decorate the corner with a birthday banner, a baby picture of each student, and a student-made graph of class birthdays. Display a 12-month calendar with birthdays written in so each child can count down to his big day. When a birthday arrives, let the birthday child sit in the special corner throughout the day. This unique arrangement will be ready each time a birthday rolls around, and students will feel honored to sit in the celebration corner.

Carolyn Walker—Gr. 2
Bettie F. Williams School
Virginia Beach, VA

Celebrate With Stories

Invite a special visitor into the classroom to help celebrate a student's day of honor. When a student's birthday rolls around, ask Mom, Dad, or an older brother or sister to select one of the student's favorite books. Invite the guest to visit the classroom to share the story with the class. After sharing the story, take a picture of the birthday child and visitor. Tape the photo inside the book cover and shelve the book in your classroom library for the remainder of the month. Students can visit the library to read their favorite stories and look over photos of special days.

Claudia Baumann—Gr. 1, Cabrillo Elementary, Hawthorne, CA

Happy Birthday to Jen.
She is a good friend.
She turns eight this year.
Let's all give a cheer!

A Special Song

Everyone hears the same ol' song on their birthday, so why don't you give it a new twist? Use the tune to the traditional birthday song to have your students compose a personalized version for the birthday child. Then surprise the child by singing the new verse following the original "Happy Birthday To You." It's such a nice surprise, you may be asked for an encore!

Rita Petrocco
Nepean, Ontario
Canada

Sweet Greeting

This easy and inexpensive birthday card will convey the sweetest of greetings. Create the card from a colored 3" x 5" index card. Write the message "Here are hugs and kisses on your birthday!" and attach a Hershey's Hug™ and Kiss™ on either side of the message. Lead the class in a rousing chorus of "Happy Birthday To You" as you present the card to the student of honor. What a tasty way to deliver birthday wishes!

Rhonda Hale—Primary Teacher
Jamestown Elementary School
Jamestown, KY

Here are hugs and kisses on your birthday!
Love,
Ms. Hale

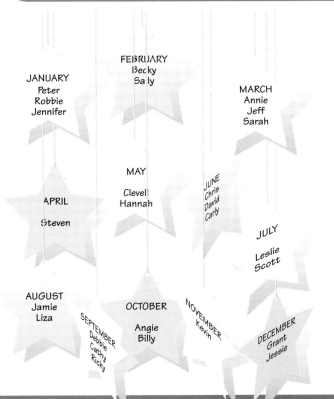

JANUARY
Peter
Robbie
Jennifer

FEBRUARY
Becky
Sally

MARCH
Annie
Jeff
Sarah

APRIL
Steven

MAY
Clevell
Hannah

JUNE
Chris
David
Carly

JULY
Leslie
Scott

AUGUST
Jamie
Liza

SEPTEMBER
Debbie
Cathy
Ricky

OCTOBER
Angie
Billy

NOVEMBER
Kevin

DECEMBER
Grant
Jessie

Star-Studded Birthdays

This heavenly birthday display will brighten your classroom instantly, yet requires only minimal preparation. Cut and laminate 12 large star shapes from yellow construction paper. Use a permanent marker to label each star with a month of the year. Then use a washable marker to program each star with the names of students having birthdays that month. For a galactic display, suspend the stars from the ceiling with monofilament line. Each student will be starstruck to see his name twinkling from above!

Leslie Poythress—Gr. 3
Gray Elementary School
Gray, GA

Birthday Beat

If you're looking for a unique way to honor a student on his birthday, try singing to him with style! Use the traditional birthday song in a variety of singing styles, such as opera (wear a tiara and sing in soprano), superman (wear a red cape and flex your muscles as you sing), cowboy (wear a cowboy hat and sing with a "countrified" twang), or baby (hold a blanket and use baby talk in the song). Students will remember this serenade for years to come!

Jeannie Hinyard—Gr. 2
Welder Elementary School
Sinton, TX

The Birthday Binder

A little preparation at the beginning of the school year can help you keep track of student birthdays all year long. During the first week of school, purchase a class supply of birthday cards. Write a birthday greeting to a student on each card and file it by month in a binder or planner that has a divider section for each month of the year. At the beginning of each month, find the appropriate section of the binder and hand out the birthday cards for the month. With this organized system, you'll be ready for everyone's special day.

Diane Fortunato—Gr. 2, Carteret School, Bloomfield, NJ

Send In The Clowns

Create a birthday atmosphere in the class with an assortment of scrap-paper clowns. Label a special box in your art center for scrap materials, and instruct students to use materials from that box for special birthday projects. On a day of celebration, add a supply of 6-inch paper plates to the center. Encourage each student to create a birthday clown face from the paper plate and materials found in the scrap box. Display the clowns in the classroom, then present them to the birthday child at the end of the day. What could be more fun than taking home a few clowns on your birthday?

Rita Petrocco
Nepean, Ontario
Canada

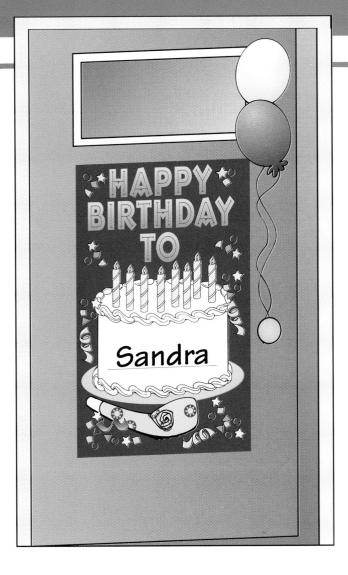

The Gift Of Books

Share the joy of reading as a special treat in honor of a student's birthday. At the beginning of the year, gift wrap a favorite book for each student in your class and place it in a large box or basket. When a student's special day arrives, have him select a book from the box, unwrap it, and sit by you as you read the story to the class. (After the story you can return the book to your private collection, if desired.) What nicer gift could there be than sharing a special story together?

Rita Petrocco
Nepean, Ontario
Canada

Happy Birthday!

Poster Pizzazz

Extend a big birthday greeting to your student of honor with a personalized birthday poster displayed on your classroom door. At the beginning of the year, create a poster bearing the message "Happy Birthday To _____," then illustrate with pictures of balloons, party favors, and candles. Laminate the completed poster. When a day of celebration rolls around, use a water-based marker to fill in the blank with the name of the birthday child. To reuse the poster, simply wipe off the student's name with a damp cloth, then reprogram with the name of the next birthday child. Imagine how special a student will feel as he enters the classroom on his big day and finds this greeting waiting at the door!

Diane Fortunato—Gr. 2
Carteret School
Bloomfield, NJ

Silhouette Similarities

Encourage your youngsters to find out how much they have in common with their classmates with this one-of-a-kind idea. Duplicate a copy of the silhouettes on page 147 for each student; then pair students. Ask each child to interview his partner to determine how they are alike and different. Instruct the child to list the attributes they have in common in the overlapping portion of the heads and different attributes on the nonoverlapping sections. Display the completed silhouettes on a classroom wall so students can locate other classmates with similarities and interesting differences.

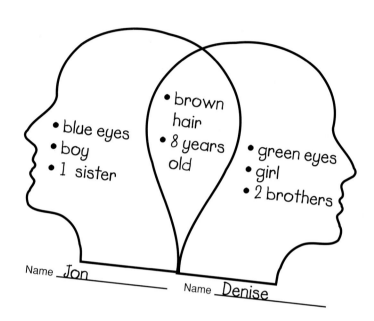

Marsha Weiner—Gr. 2
Churchill School
Homewood, IL

Special Letters

Children say and do the cutest things. Use this tip to help capture these memories. At the beginning of the school year, write the name of each student on a separate page of a small notebook. Keep the notebook in an accessible location. Throughout the year, jot down witty comments and sweet compliments that you hear and special things that you see each child do. At the end of the year, use your notes to write each child a farewell letter that includes the many special things she has done. Your students will be surprised and delighted to know how much they've touched your heart, not to mention what a good memory you have!

Nancy Lujan—Gr. 3
C. I. Waggoner Elementary School
Tempe, AZ

Nicole Hall

9–17 said school is her favorite place

10–1 befriended the new girl in the class

Feeling Good About Me!

Give your students the chance to show off with these praiseworthy posters. Provide each child with a piece of poster board. Instruct each child to write his full name at the top of the poster using different colored markers. Each week have students add descriptive words or phrases of themselves to their posters. Descriptions might include likes and dislikes, possible future careers, hobbies, or family pictures. After the descriptions have been added, have students decorate their posters with glitter and sequins. Then display the posters in the hall so everyone can see what a positive group of youngsters you have!

Cindy Ward—Grs. 1–4
Learning Disabilities Teacher
Yellow Branch School
Rustburg, VA

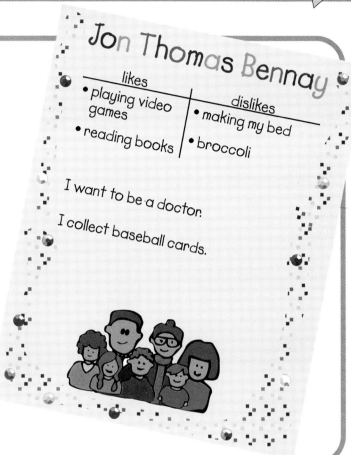

"Power" Lunch

Show your students how much you care by inviting them to lunch once a month. Set aside the last Friday in each month for a "power" lunch. Instead of eating in the cafeteria, have students take their lunches to the classroom or outside for a picnic. Play soft background music and provide dessert, if desired. Top off the lunch with a big thank-you to your students for all that they have accomplished during the month. Students will enjoy eating their lunches in style and will surely be energized and ready for more work after this powerful lunch date!

Susan Hastings—Gr. 3
Sheffield Elementary
Turners Falls, MA

Star Of The Week

Give your student star of the week the chance to shine extra brightly! In addition to the personal memorabilia that she brings to school for her week in the spotlight, ask her to complete a copy of the star report on page 148. Display the completed report, along with the student's personal effects, a large personalized construction-paper star, and family photographs, at your star-of-the-week exhibit. Your students will enjoy learning about their special classmate and she will relish her time in the limelight. What better way to foster a glowing self-esteem!

Debra Dahl—Gr. 2
St. Charles Primary School
Chippewa Falls, WI

An Extraspecial Delivery!

Use this tip to show your students how much you care and add a little beauty to your classroom at the same time. On special occasions purchase bouquets of flowers for your youngsters and ask a co-worker to deliver them to the classroom. Be sure that each table gets a bouquet and an attached card with students' names on it. Provide vases or tall jars for the flowers. Students will reminisce about this delivery time and time again!

Sarah Mertz—Grs. 1–2, Owenton, KY

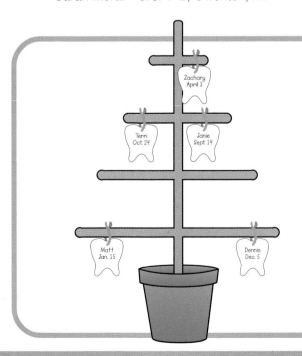

Tooth Tree

Youngsters look forward to losing their teeth, so why not create a display that highlights this experience for them? Purchase a miniature tree from a craft store. When a child loses a tooth, ask him to sign his name and write the date on a tooth cutout. Punch a hole at the top of the cutout, thread a length of yarn through the hole, and tie the yarn into a loop. Have the child hang his tooth from a tree branch. By the end of the year, the tree will be covered with pearly whites!

Linda Davis—Gr. 1
St. Mark School
Indianapolis, IN

A Letter-Perfect Class

Boost self-esteem and reinforce adjectives at the same time with this nifty activity. In advance, cut out a large, block letter of each child's first initial. Ask your students to brainstorm adjectives to describe themselves. Record their responses on chart paper. Next instruct each child to use a marker to write his first name near the top of his letter cutout. Then have him write several adjectives that describe himself, referring to the chart if needed. Have children search in magazines and newspapers for pictures or other words that tell about themselves. Instruct students to glue these on their letters. Display the completed letter cutouts around the classroom to remind your students just how wonderful they are. Children will beam with pride and learn about others, too!

Kristin Moritz—Gr. 2
Park Elementary
Columbia, PA

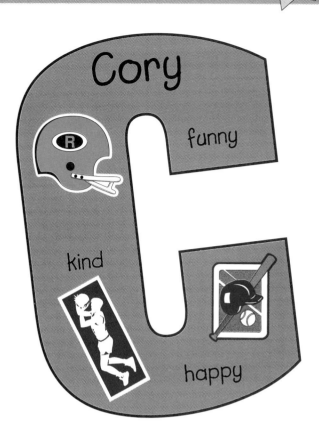

A Basket Of Feelings

Help youngsters develop a larger "feeling vocabulary" with a basket of feeling words. Write several different feelings, such as "mad" and "embarrassed," on craft sticks and then place them in a basket. To begin the activity, gather students in a circle on the floor. Hand the basket to one student and have him select a stick. The child reads the feeling word, explains a time when he felt that way, and then places the stick back in the basket. Have the students pass the basket around the circle until each student has had a turn. Add other emotions, such as "confused" and "disappointed," to the craft sticks and repeat the activity later in the year. It won't take long for students to realize that everyone experiences a wide range of emotions.

Cindy Ward—Grs. 1–4
Learning Disabilities Teacher
Yellow Branch Elementary School
Rustburg, VA

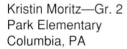

Artist Of The Week

Spotlight youngsters' artwork with this special display. Each week place a student's artwork in a large picture frame. Mount the frame and a corresponding caption outside your classroom door along with a labeled photograph of the featured artist. Then mount a piece of poster board and some pencils below the picture so passersby and classmates can write compliments about the drawing. Your little artists will be all grins when they read the compliments written by their schoolmates!

Name Meanings

Help students realize just how special they are by holding a class study of names and meanings. In advance, check out a book of baby names (with their meanings) from your public library. Ask a student to share with the class what she thinks her name means; then read the meaning from the book. Continue in this manner until each child has had a turn. Next place the book at a center so students can write down the meanings of their family members' names. Have students share the meanings with their families as a homework assignment.

Awards Day

Don't wait until the end of the school year to have an awards day—have one once a week! On Friday pass out blank awards, and let each child give himself an award. Have the student select either a skill that he has done well or a good quality that he has shown. Sign the awards and have students take them home to share with their parents. Students will learn how to self-evaluate and in turn be more aware of their strengths and weaknesses. A variation is for students to give awards to each other. Either way students will go home smiling every Friday!

Curb Hurtful Words

Remind your students how hurtful words can be with this hands-on activity that requires only a tube of toothpaste and a paper plate. Have a volunteer squeeze all the toothpaste from the tube and onto a paper plate. Compare that easy task to how easy it is to say hurtful words, such as "I don't like you" or "You can't play." Next ask for another volunteer. Instruct the student to make the toothpaste go back to the way it was by putting it back into the tube. Once the students realize it can't be done, remind the children again that hurtful words can't be taken back or forgotten. Students are sure to squeeze the meaning out of this activity, which will lead to a happier classroom!

Rhonda Hale—Primary
Jamestown Elementary
Jamestown, KY

The Compliment Game

This special game teaches children to appreciate themselves and others. Write the word "Me" on five cards, "You" on five cards, and "Super Star" on one card. Place the cards in a container. To play, have students sit in a circle. Pass the container to the first student. If he draws a "Me" card, the student must say something nice about himself. If he draws a "You" card, he must say something nice about the person to his left. If he draws the "Super Star" card *everyone* must say something nice about *him*. Be sure students return cards to the container before passing it on. Continue playing until each child has had a turn. Be sure to take a turn yourself!

Personalized Windsocks

Encourage youngsters to appreciate their unique qualities by making personalized windsocks. In advance, cut off the bottom fourth of a small lunch bag for each student. Instruct each child to write words to describe himself on all four sides of the bag; then have him draw small pictures to accompany the words. Next have the student glue strips of crepe paper streamers around the inside of the bottom of the bag. To complete the windsock, assist the child in making two small holes at the top of his bag and threading a pipe cleaner through to create a handle. Display throughout the classroom to brighten up the windiest of days!

Marsha Weiner—Gr. 2
Churchill School
Homewood, IL

Photocopy Pizzazz

Promote self-esteem and add pizzazz to your photocopies at the same time! Before duplicating a reproducible for your students, add a photocopy of one of your student's school pictures. Duplicate and distribute student copies; then watch for astonished faces as students discover the featured classmate. Keep a list of the students whose photos have been featured so that every child has a turn. For a variation, decorate reproducibles with small student drawings. What better way to brighten up reproducibles than with your youngsters' smiling faces and beautiful artwork!

Super Students

Help students focus on the positive points of their classmates with this activity. Each week choose a person to be the super student of the week. To honor the student, ask her classmates to brainstorm special attributes about the person. Record their responses on chart paper. Instruct each student to write a letter to the super student, using the ideas on the chart if needed. Encourage students to use the rules for writing a friendly letter, using the correct punctuation, and practicing their neatest handwriting. Display the completed letters on a specially decorated bulletin board throughout the week; then send the letters home with the super student on Friday. Students will enjoy the chance to honor a classmate and will look forward to their special week!

Jill Lieberman—Gr. 2
Bedford Village Elementary School
Bedford, NY

Dear Nicole,
You are a good listener.
I like the pictures you draw.

Your friend,
Katie

The "I Can" Can

Set your students up for some ego boosting with this noteworthy idea. Decorate a coffee can and label it "I Can." Ask students to brainstorm skills that they can do now but could not do at the beginning of the year. Have each student choose one item and write it on a strip of paper. Place the strips in the can. Throughout the year have students write their accomplishments on strips of paper and place them in the can. Once the can is full, reward your students with a special treat. If desired, ask for volunteers to read some of their accomplishments. Students will be amazed at their many successes and realize that successes come in cans—not cannots!

Joann Bollinger—Gr. 3
Plains Elementary School
Timberville, VA

I can write my name in cursive.

Ann Coleman

Unstuck Papers

Tired of students' cut-and-paste papers sticking to each other? Here's a solution to these sticky situations! Add a magnet to each student's list of school supplies. Or, if desired, make a personalized magnet for each student as a welcome-to-school present. Ask each child to keep his magnet stuck to the side of his desk or to the chalkboard. Whenever he completes an activity that requires glue, he uses the magnet to hang the paper to dry. At the end of the day, the student removes his dried paper and stacks it in the turn-in basket to be graded. Now that's a solution you can stick with!

Pat Biancardi—Gr. 2, Homan Elementary School
Schererville, IN

Positive Note Box

To ease the important job of sending notes home, try this organizational tip. Duplicate a supply of various kinds of positive notes that can be sent home, such as notes for outstanding behavior or handwriting improvement. Label a file folder for each type of note; then place the files in a crate or decorated box. File the notes in their appropriate folders. When you need an award, simply pull one from the file and add any additional information. Parents and students will be delighted with the arrival of these positive notes!

Patti Devall—Gr. 3, St. Anthony Grade School, Effingham, IL

The True Story Of The
Three Little Pigs
by Jon Scieszka
- personal
- Nov. (writing unit – who,
what, when, where)

Story-Time File

Keep information about your favorite read-aloud books organized with a personalized card system. On an index card, write the title and author of each book; then note where this book can be found (school library, public library, personal collection) and the time of year you usually read it. On the back of the card, list activities that you've done to accompany the story. Put the cards in a recipe box on your desk to keep the information at your fingertips. After sharing a book with the class, place its card behind a divider labeled "Read This School Year." At the end of the school year, simply move the divider behind the last card and you're ready for next year.

New Students

It's inevitable! More than likely you'll get a new student during the middle of the school year. Use this organizational tip to help you and your newcomer settle in a little easier! At the beginning of the year, reproduce extra copies of all necessary classroom information such as class schedules, lunch forms, and a first-day welcome note. Place the information in folders labeled "Welcome To Our Class." Store the folders along with any needed textbooks on a shelf. Whenever a new student arrives, you'll be ready to greet her with a warm smile and the needed supplies to start off her first day just right!

Janet Zeek—Gr. 2, Tolleson Elementary School
Tolleson, AZ

Color Copies

This color-coded system allows you to organize your reproducibles, therefore making them easier to identify. Decide on a specific color of duplicating paper for reproducibles in each subject area. For example math copies could be green; science copies, blue; and language arts copies, pink. Throughout the year, duplicate reproducibles in each subject area on their specific colored paper. To help get even more organized, choose a color of paper to use for all correspondence sent to parents. Now that your reproducibles are organized, your days will surely be brighter!

Peter Tucciarone—Gr. 3, Rowan Elementary
Cranberry Township, PA

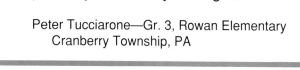

Bulletin-Board Notebook

Do you have trouble remembering past bulletin boards? If so, try this idea! Take a photograph of each new bulletin board; then glue each photograph to an 8 1/2" x 11" piece of paper. Or, when you find a new bulletin-board idea in *The Mailbox®*, duplicate a copy of the idea. File the pages in a three-ring binder. Use index dividers to organize the patterns by month or subject area. Now when you need an idea for a bulletin board, it will be neatly organized and easily accessible to you and helpful parent volunteers!

Patti Devall—Gr. 3
St. Anthony Grade School
Effingham, IL

Storing Letter Cutouts

Here's a quick tip for organizing your bulletin-board letters. Label a file folder for each letter of the alphabet, punctuation, and numbers; then place the alphabetized folders in a crate or decorated box. Sort bulletin-board letters into their appropriate folders. Store the crate in a handy location. The next time you need letter cutouts, you'll have them neatly organized and ready to use! When it's time to return the cutouts to their files, you're sure to have students volunteering to do the chore.

Patti Devall—Gr. 3

Crate It!

Eliminate those last-minute struggles to collect materials for lessons with this handy tip. Label a file folder for each day of the school week. Store the folders in a crate. On Friday afternoon, consult your lesson plans for the coming week. Take a few minutes to gather all of the materials needed for each day. Place flash cards, charts, seat work, and other needed teaching materials in the appropriate folder for the day. Your materials crate will be a tremendous help to you, as well as a substitute teacher!

Melissa Woody—Substitute Teacher
Bedford North Lawrence Community Schools
Bedford, IN

Album Of Ideas

Keep your favorite teaching ideas within easy reach with this great tip. As you read teacher resource books, photocopy your favorite art ideas, time-fillers, classroom activities, and other teaching tips. Organize and label them by subject to fit into a large photo album. Store the photo album in a convenient location so that terrific ideas are right at your fingertips.

Beth Fondale—Gr. 2, St. Rose School, Junction City, OH

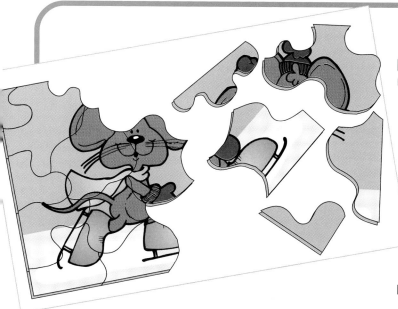

Puzzle Pleasers

Puzzled about how to keep unfinished puzzles in place when they are not being used? Then this is the idea for you! Place a self-adhesive strip on the back of each puzzle piece. Then have students work the puzzle on a magnetic surface. Now when students have to leave a puzzle before they are finished working, they are assured the puzzle will stay in place until they can return to complete it. What a pleasing thought—no more jumbled puzzles!

Deborah Ross—Primary Teacher, Wayland Alexander School, Hartford, KY

Grade-Book Tip

To keep track of returned homework assignments, try this colorful technique. When a student turns in a completed homework assignment, use a green-colored pencil to color a block in the grade book beside his name. If the student does not complete the homework on time, color the block red. Once the homework is complete, use a black pen to mark in the red block the number of days the assignment is late. A red block without a number means the homework was never completed. This color-coded method of keeping track of homework makes it easy to check at a quick glance who has or has not been completing homework.

Liesl Collins—Gr. 3
Littleton Elementary School
Cashion, AZ

name	Math p. 1	Math p. 10	Math p. 21	Math p. 23	Math p. 24
Kenny					
Georgia	1	1			
Rodney			2		
Frankie		2			
Lara			1		
Barbara					
Charles					
Jayne	2				

Nightly Homework Calendar

These homework calendars help students and their parents anticipate homework assignments—and the best part of all is that students make up the homework! At the end of the month, tell students the themes that will be studied next month. Provide each child with an index card. Instruct him to write his name and a short homework assignment on the card. Collect the cards and program a calendar with each child's assignment and name in a calendar square. Duplicate a copy of the calendar for each child to take home at the beginning of the month. Students will develop a more positive attitude about homework now that they give the assignments!

Deborah Ross—Primary Teacher
Wayland Alexander School
Hartford, KY

12 Stephen M.
Tell about a time you were either really scared or really happy.

14 Katie H.
Create a picture using shapes. Don't forget to color it.

May

				1 Richie M.	2 Caroline
4 Charles S.	5 Barbara P.	6 Chris H.	7 Miriam M.	8 Nichlaus P.	9 Sophie B.	10 Christine R.
11 Joey S.	12 Stephen M.	13 David H.	14 Katie H.	15 Rodney L.	16 Jay P.	17 Georgia R.
18 Jayne G.	19 Sean A.	20 Andrew L.	21 Taylor D.	22 Lauren K.	23 Mandy P.	24 Danielle H.
25 Luke B.	26 Frances T.	27 Meredith A.	28 Stacey A.	29 Nicholas G.	30 Dana P.	31 Heather M.

Poetry Storage

Here's a quick and easy way to store poems on chart paper. Clip them to skirt hangers and store the hangers on a chart stand. Hang additional poems on other skirt hangers. To keep the hangers from sliding off the chart stand, put a dab of Sticky-Tac on each side of the hangers. When you're in need of a poem, flip through the hangers to view your selection with a quick glance. What a relief—no more lost or damaged poetry charts!

Susan Baker—Gr. 2
Sawgrass Elementary
Sunrise, FL

A Place for Everything

Tired of hearing those words, "What do I do with this?" Set up three paper trays on a table near your desk. Label one tray "Notes for the teacher," one tray "Homework," and the other tray "Classwork." Have students place communications and assignments in these trays.

Storage Chests

Use storage chests to bring organization to your classroom in a variety of ways. Organize game pieces by attaching two matching sticky dots: one to a gameboard and the other to one drawer of the chest. Label each pair of dots with the same number. Store all the game's pieces in the labeled drawer. Organize grading stickers by labeling each drawer with a different type of sticker; then sort the stickers into the drawers. Storage chests can also be used to organize math manipulatives such as dice, counters, and plastic coins. Both you and your students will have a much easier time locating materials, and that means more time available for games and learning!

Getting Organized

No More Knots

If you have a listening center in your classroom, then this is the tip for you! Mount a sturdy towel bar on the wall nearest your listening center. Using colored sticky dots, label the headsets and the towel bar with corresponding colors. Then label the outlets at the listening center with the same color code. A student identifies the color-coded outlet that is nearest him and removes the matching headset from the bar. At the end of the activity, he returns the headset to its appropriate location. Now that you're not spending time getting knots out of headsets, you'll have more time where it's needed—teaching the students!

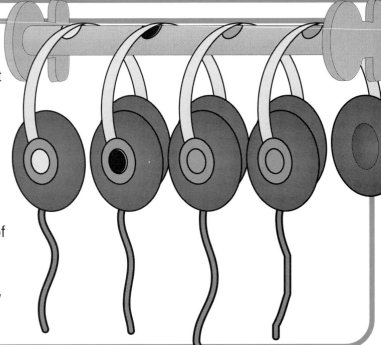

Theme Organization

Two thumbs up for this idea for organizing your thematic units. Label a folder with pockets for each unit of study. Use the folders to store sample worksheets, brochures, art projects, and other various materials relating to the themes. Store a piece of notebook paper in one pocket of the folder to note related activities, bulletin boards, books, and films. This system makes it simple to get what you need, when you need it, year after year.

Beth Fondale—Gr. 2, St. Rose School, Junction City, OH

The Three Little Goats

by Chris Speckman

Brave Soldier

by Caroline Smith

Hang It Up!

Having trouble finding room to display your collection of picture books? If so, try this idea! Attach a row of self-adhesive hooks below the chalkboard. Place a large rubber band in the middle of each book as shown. Then suspend each book by its rubber band from a hook. No more stacking books on tables or putting them in baskets. Students will be able to view the enticing covers of many books at one time.

Deborah Ross—Primary Teacher
Wayland Elementary School
Hartford, KY

Anecdotal Note File

Need some help organizing and keeping daily information on each child? Try this easy and inexpensive technique. Place the top of a 5" x 8" lined index card near the bottom edge of an open folder. Tape the card in place as shown. Place a second card on top of the first one, matching its top edge to the first line of the first card. Tape the second card in place. Continue adding a card for each child, using both sides of the open folder. Label each card with a student's name. Every student's card is now at your fingertips for recording strengths and weaknesses on a daily basis. One file may be used for all subjects, or if desired, make a file for each subject. These cards will be of great value for report cards and parent conferences.

Scrap Paper Saver

Save that scrap paper! It's a valuable resource for a variety of projects. To organize these often messy scraps, position a cardboard shoe organizer vertically. Fold various colors of large construction-paper sheets in half to use as folders. Stand these colored folders in the slots of the organizer. Store your scraps of paper in the corresponding colored folders. Label each slot with the colors of folders it contains. Then when your students need construction paper for projects, they simply remove the desired colors from the folders and place the folders back in the organizer. If desired, assign a student each week to make sure the folders are neatly put away. What a great way to recycle and keep your art center clean!

Noise-Level Signal

Remind students to be quiet using this traffic signal. Make a large stoplight cutout. Color three black circles down the middle. Add one hook to each circle. Cut out three circles to fit the traffic light—one green, one yellow, and one red. Suspend the red construction-paper circle from its hook to indicate silent time, the yellow circle for whisper time, and the green circle for talk freely time. If desired, create a student job titled "traffic controller." His job would be to change the color of the light at your signal. This traffic theme is sure to have your youngsters cooperatively working towards a green-light classroom!

Lauren Egizio—Substitute Teacher
Easton Public Schools
Easton, MA

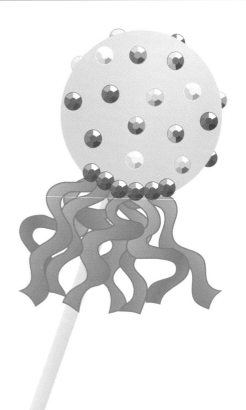

The Magic Wand

Take the "shh!" out of your vocabulary with this magical tip. Let students know it's group time by waving a magic wand over each student's head. To make a wand, push a Styrofoam® ball into one end of a three-inch dowel. Spray paint both the ball and the dowel gold. Then use hot glue to attach sequins and metallic ribbons to the wand. At the end of the year, invite each student to make her own magic wand as a special memento of a great school year. What a difference a little magic makes!

Linda Cooper—Gr. 2
North Londonderry Elementary School
Londonderry, NH

Credit Cards For Success

No annual fee, no finance charges, and rewards—just the kind of credit cards your students need. Issue a 3 1/2" x 2" piece of poster board to each child. Have students use markers to decorate and personalize their credit cards. Whenever a student earns a good grade or displays good behavior, punch a hole on his card. Once a predetermined number of holes has been punched, the student redeems his card for a special treat. Students will be motivated to do their best work since they know it applies to their credit.

Tracie Smithwick-Rodriguez—Gr. 2
Lexington Elementary School
Corpus Christi, TX

CREDIT CARD
Betty Ann Holding

35 free-time minutes

Today Is Double-Minutes Day!

Minute Madness

Every minute counts with this motivational tip. To keep students quiet in the halls, during special classes, and at other appropriate times during the day, offer extra minutes of free time. For example, each time students walk quietly in the halls, add three minutes to their free-choice time. (Keep a running total on the chalkboard.) Then on Friday afternoon provide students with their earned minutes of free time. For added motivation, occasionally declare "Double-Minutes Day."

Peggy Morin—Gr. 2
Miller School
Wilton, CT

Problem Report

Use problem reports to take care of a major classroom problem—tattling. When children feel they need to report an incident, instead of running to tell you, they each fill out a problem report (see page 149) and turn it in to a predetermined basket. Look over it immediately to make sure it is not urgent. If it is not urgent, wait until just before recess to go through the reports, dealing only with the reports that are completely filled in. Ask each child who filled out a report if he would still like to deal with the problem. If so, meet privately with the students involved. By this time, students will have had time to think through the incident and will perhaps be more willing to consider other perspectives. Review the situation with the students involved, determine the consequences, and then have the students sign the forms. File the forms to use as a reference during parent communications.

P. J. Myers—Gr. 3
W. R. V. Worthington Elementary/Junior High School
Worthington, IN

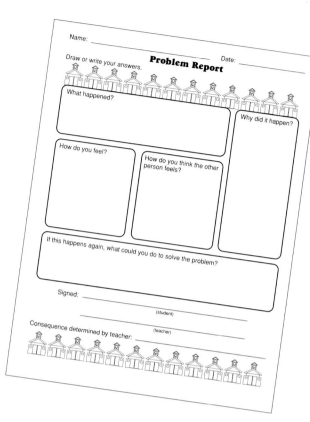

Buddy Cards

Do your students gravitate to the same classmates during group activities? Then try this tip! Personalize an index card for each student. Randomly place the name cards on students' desks. Have students sit wherever they find their name cards. Not only do students learn to cooperatively work with others; they're gaining buddies, too!

Cindy Ward—Grs. 1–4
Learning Disabilities Teacher
Yellow Branch Elementary
Rustburg, VA

Check The Mailbox!

Notices to be sent home with students are often forgotten. Not anymore! Post a mailbox labeled "Don't Forget!" beside your classroom exit door. When you have handouts to send home with your students, place them in the mailbox and raise the flag. It won't take long for students to get in the habit of checking the mail each day as they leave school. And that means no more forgotten notes!

Deb Olson—Grs. K–2
Gates School
Broken Bow, NE

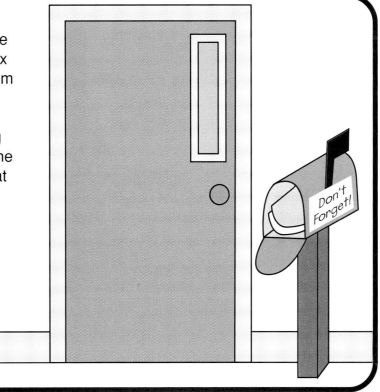

A Colorful Collection Of Desks

Use color-coded student desks to help manage your classroom in a variety of ways! You will need construction-paper circles or self-adhesive dots in six different colors. Arrange your students' desks in groups of six; then attach a different color of circle or dot to each desk in a group. When it's time to distribute materials, call out one of the six colors and you'll have a representative from each group to help you. During cooperative learning activities you can quickly assign jobs by making a color choice. Or use the color code when it's time to collect materials or clean up the classroom. What a simple solution to an often difficult and time-consuming task!

Ron Derr—Gr. 3
Brecknock Elementary
Shillington, PA

Magic Pencil Day

Do your students spend too much of their time grinding their pencils away at the pencil sharpener? Then this is the tip for you! Supply each child with a sharpened, personalized pencil. Explain to your students that every few weeks you will randomly declare "Magic Pencil Day." Each student who still has a good portion of his personalized pencil remaining on that day will receive a special treat. Students will stop sharpening their pencils unnecessarily, and they'll keep better track of them, too!

Donna Vandiver—Gr. 2
Mary Ford Elementary
North Charleston, SC

Numbers, Numbers Everywhere!

Assigning student identification numbers can save you time and energy in many different ways. Assign each student a different number, according to the alphabetized name list in your grade book. Instead of writing each child's name on his folders, books, and pencils, save time by writing only his number. Student numbers are also helpful when collecting assignments. Have each student write his number on all his assignments. (If desired designate a specific location for student numbers to be written.) When collecting assignments, place them in numerical order. At a glance you can see which numbers are missing and refer to your grade book for their names.

Wrenda Rogers Whitley—Gr. 1
Mtn. View Elementary
Hays, NC

Stop And Think

Students learn to monitor their own behavior with this eye-catching, classroom traffic light. You will need a personalized clothespin for each student and one red, one yellow, and one green plastic plate (or white paper plates covered with construction paper). To make the traffic light, glue the three plates to a yardstick as shown. At the beginning of the day, each student's clothespin starts out clipped to the green light. If the child receives a warning for inappropriate behavior, have him move his clothespin to the yellow light. If the misbehavior continues, have the student move his clothespin to the red light, and proceed with appropriate discipline. The traffic light serves as a visual reminder for students to stop and think before they act.

Leslie Poythress—Gr. 3
Gray Elementary School
Gray, GA

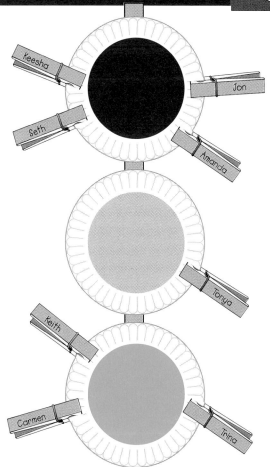

Promoting Quality Work

This incentive program motivates students to do their best work. Personalize a bear cutout for each student; then display them on a classroom wall titled " 'Bearly' An Error." Award each student one sticker for each perfect paper that he completes. If desired, provide a special treat or privilege for each student who collects a predetermined number of stickers.

Each month cut out new bears with seasonal accessories (such as Halloween masks in October, graduation caps in May, etc.). Be sure to send the bears from the previous month home with your students for their parents to view. Before you know it, your youngsters will be doing their 'beary' best work all of the time!

Phyllis Bowling—Gr. 2
Smithville Elementary
Smithville, MS

Free-Time Folders

Looking for a way to eliminate the phrase "What do I do now?" from your students' vocabularies? Here's an idea for you. Personalize a two-pocket folder for each child. Then fill each child's folder with individualized, enrichment activities. Include items such as crossword puzzles, word searches, logic problems, story starters, and seasonal activities. When a student completes an assignment, she looks in her folder and chooses a free-time activity. Periodically check each child's folder to see if new activities are needed. Now your early birds who fly through assignments have a special treat to keep them busy.

Andrea Hunter—Gr. 1
Fullington Academy
Pinehurst, GA

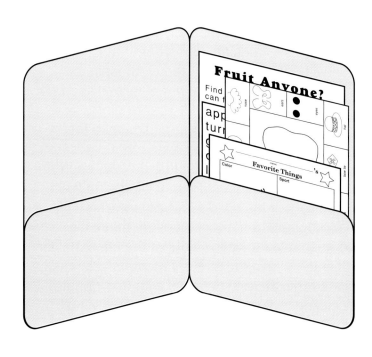

Lost BUT Found!

It never fails—students are always losing things and interrupting lessons to tell you. Help students keep track of their personal items with a lost-and-found box. Decorate a small box and label it "Lost BUT Found!" Whenever students find or lose an item, they can head directly to the box. Children get their possessions back without interrupting you, which means more time to teach.

Esther Gaines—Gr. 2
Sabal Palm Elementary
North Miami Beach, FL

No Hassle Lineup

Lining students up to go somewhere can be hectic at times. Keep your students in the right spots with this idea. Cut out a class supply of shoe shapes. Label shoe cutouts for the line leader and door holder. Label the other shoe cutouts with numbers or letters of the alphabet. Place the cutouts in their correct order in line and then cover them with clear Con-Tact® paper. To use this line-up system, assign each student a number or letter. Whenever it's time to go somewhere, simply have students stand in line on their assigned numbers or job names. (When students have line jobs, their numbered shoes stay empty.) To add variety, periodically change students' numbers throughout the year. There you have it—a no hassle technique to line students up. What a relief!

Amy Ruff—Gr. 2
Inman Elementary
Inman, SC

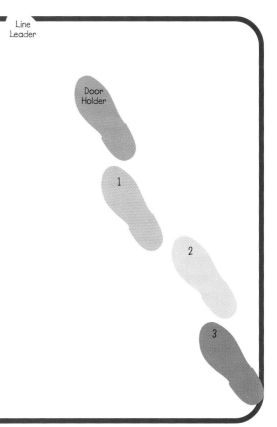

Recreational Reading In The Bag

To make recreational-reading time more efficient, have students prepare their books in advance. Sort your classroom library into three sections of books—easy, average, and difficult. Give each category of books a color code; then attach a matching-colored sticky dot to the spine of each book. Label a bookshelf for each section and place each book on the appropriate shelf.

Have each child choose books from his assigned shelf and store his books for recreational-reading time in a large, resealable plastic bag. When it comes time for recreational reading, each child can take the bag from his desk and begin reading with no delays. At the end of the day, each student sets his empty bag on his desk. As students arrive the next morning, the empty bags will remind them to select new books.

Amy Ruff—Gr. 2

Lots Of Pointers

Catch your students' attention by making your own pointers and lots of them! Purchase several 1/4" dowels and cut them in half. Use a hot glue gun to attach a lightweight object to the end of each dowel. Choose a theme-related object, such as a plastic shark when studying the ocean or a toy car when studying transportation. If you are unable to find a suitable object, then use a photograph or picture. Mount the picture on tagboard, laminate, and then trim off the excess. To really add some interest in your classroom, make a pointer with a picture of your principal holding his arm up. Now that's sure to get your students to the point of the lesson.

Sarah Mertz—Grs. 1–2
Owenton, KY

Desk Fairy

Just in time—a great idea for motivating students to keep their desks clean. Explain to your youngsters that a Desk Fairy comes by once a week after school to check for clean desks. The Desk Fairy leaves a special treat, such as sugarless gum or an eraser, for all the students who have clean desks. Since students never know what day the Desk Fairy is coming, they'll keep their desks always looking their best!

Deb Olson—Grs. K–2
Gates School
Broken Bow, NE

Do-Now Assignments

Start your day in an organized way! Each morning write a joke and a list of three to four short assignments on the chalkboard. Students complete the tasks whenever they have extra time, such as before the morning bell rings or after lunch. The students will look forward to the joke and the unpredictability of the tasks, and you will have time to tend to messages from parents or to work with students needing individualized help.

Jane Oliva—Gr. 2
St. Robert Bellarmine School
Bayside, NY

What do cows do when they meet?
They have a milk shake.

1. Journal writing
2. Math sheet on addition
3. Use each spelling word in a
   sentence.

100
It was fun when we had the
Multicultural Fair. My favorite part
was listening to the marimba band.
It made it seem like we were in
America.

Tracey's
Portfolio

Assignments Worth A Smile

Help students gather portfolios full of smiley faces with this one-of-a-kind idea. Each week, place assignments in a basket as you grade them. On Friday distribute the graded papers to your students. Have each child review her assignments to decide which papers to include in her portfolio. Provide students with yellow, smiley face stickers to place in the top right corner of each paper they choose to go in their portfolios. Before placing students' papers in their portfolios, have students take their papers home for their parents to review and return to school the next day. Parents will appreciate the chance to look at their child's work before too much time has passed. (Send a note home explaining this portfolio technique so parents will know that assignments with yellow stickers need to be returned to school.) Students will enjoy evaluating their own work and you'll spend less time dealing with portfolios.

Marlaena Perron—Gr. 2, Forest Glen Elementary, Green Bay, WI

Bathroom Bear

Know at a glance which student is taking a restroom break by providing a bathroom bear for your students. Decorate a small wooden bear and label it "Bathroom Bear." (A stuffed bear works well also.) When a child leaves to visit the restroom, he quietly places the wooden bear on his desk, then replaces the bear when he returns. Your days of wondering which student is in the bathroom are over!

Janet S. Brochu—Gr. R/1
Greenville Elementary School
Greenville, NH

1. Journal entry
2. Reading log
3. Spelling practice
4. Problem-solving booklet
5. Handwriting lesson
6. Centers

Weekly Work

Get your students organized with this tip for keeping track of weekly assignments. At the beginning of the week, tape a seasonal or theme-shaped cutout to each student's desk. Then write the weekly assignments on the chalkboard, assigning a number to each assignment. Have students write each number on his cut-out shape. When a student completes an assignment, provide him with a star sticker to place on the assignment's number. At the end of the week, reward students who covered all their numbers with a special treat or privilege. For students who did not complete their assignments, record the uncovered numbers to use as documentation for progress reports and parent conferences. Students will be motivated to do their work and they'll increase their independent work skills, too.

Deborah L. Ross—Primary
Wayland Alexander School
Hartford, KY

Who's Next?

You'll flip over this idea to minimize questions about who has and has not taken his turn at the classroom computer. Purchase a spiral-bound, index-card notebook for each computer in your classroom. Divide your students into as many groups as there are computers. Write each group of students' names in a separate notebook; then place each notebook at a different computer. To determine which students visit the computers, open each notebook to the first name. When these students complete their computer work, they flip their notebooks to the next page and inform the appropriate classmates. If one of the classmates is unavailable, the student clips a clothespin to that student's page in the notebook and flips to the next page. When the absent child returns, he will be first to take a turn at the computer. After all the students' names have been flipped through, simply return to the beginning of the book and begin again.

Erin M. Hoffman—Gr. 3
Brecknock Elementary School
Shillington, PA

Alex

Computer Border

This teacher-created computer border will prove to be a lifesaver! To make the border, measure the area of the classroom computer monitor. Cut out the measured area from a piece of poster board and then laminate. Attach the border to the monitor with Velcro®. Use a wipe-off marker to write computer rules, directions, and assignments on the border. When you're ready to change programs, simply wipe off the border with a damp cloth and reprogram. Students are never left wondering what to do at the computer again!

Tracie Smithwick-Rodriguez—Gr. 2
Lexington Elementary
Corpus Christi, TX

Do not change disks.

Play Phonics Friends, game A.

Picture-Perfect Attendance

Picture your morning attendance routine requiring little time and effort! This simple picture chart will do just that. Using a commercially made pocket chart, attach each student's photograph to the front of a pocket. As each child enters the room every morning, simply have him place a colored index card behind his picture. At a glance, you will know who is present and who is absent. Now that will put a smile on your face!

Tracey Miller—Grs. 1–2
Warfield Elementary
Indiantown, FL

Attendance With A Twist

Develop student involvement with this twist to attendance taking. Create a laminated nametag for each student using a shape cutout. Before class begins each morning, write a yes-or-no statement on the chalkboard such as, "The equator is an imaginary line that runs north and south." Provide "yes" and "no" columns near the question for students to record their answers. As each student arrives, he places his nametag under the column that represents his answer. You can easily verify who is absent and those students' names can be written on the attendance record.

Helen D. Gromadzki—Grs. 1–3
Bollman Bridge Elementary School
Jessup, MD

Mt. Rushmore is in South Dakota.

Yes | No

Tim

Molly

Erla

Nicki

Easy Daily Record Keeping

To cut down on time-consuming morning duties, have your students manage two of the daily record-keeping tasks on their own. Prepare a lunch count area that will double as an attendance record on a bulletin board or wall. Display a school lunch menu, lunch slips for the office, and a student sign-up chart. Divide the chart into columns labeled with the lunch choices, such as school lunch options and sack lunch. As each student enters the classroom in the morning, have him write his name under his lunch choice. Then it's easy to complete the lunch record for the office by glancing at the chart. By counting the names, your attendance is also quickly determined.

Erin M. Hoffman—Gr. 3
Brecknock Elementary School
Shillington, PA

Today's Menu

FIRST CHOICE	SECOND CHOICE
hamburger	baked chicken
fries	creamed potatoes
salad	peas
peaches	roll
milk	apple pie
	milk

LUNCH COUNT

first choice	second choice	sack lunch
Jeff	Sharon	Kevin
Cindy	Chad	
	Eric	

LUNCH POCKETS

Chicken Nuggets	Eric	Tom	John
	B__	Taylor	Rhane
Hamburger	Brad	Anne	Kim
	Brad	Casey	
Box Lunch	Tina	David	

Lunch Pockets

Speed up your morning routine by creating a Lunch Pocket chart. Make or purchase a pocket chart and add the title "Lunch Pockets" to the top. Then create laminated nametags for each child using a shaped notepad. Along the left column of pockets, place cards with the day's lunch choices, including an option for sack lunch. As each student arrives in the morning have her place her nametag in the row representing her lunch choice. After everyone has arrived and marked her choice, you have a clear graph showing the number of students choosing each lunch. Start your day with a short math review of graphing, rather than spending time taking a lunch count.

Laura Reeder—Gr. 2
Sara Collins Elementary
Greenville, SC

Easy ABCs

This simple tip has valuable timesaving potential! When you collect papers from students, assign a class leader to alphabetize them. After you finish checking the assignment, it's simple to enter the grades in your alphabetized gradebook because the papers are already in order. This also lends itself to easy filing in student portfolios if the portfolios are stored alphabetically.

Andrea Hunter—Gr. 1
Fullington Academy
Pinehurst, GA

Lesson Plans On Tape

Save time and energy by tape-recording lesson plans for your substitute. You can give her more information in less time and eliminate most of the writing. The recorded lesson plans are also great for leaving a "be on your best behavior" message to your students. Ask the substitute to play the message at the beginning of the day. The sound of your voice will speak volumes to your students.

Quick Return

Make it easy for colleagues to return borrowed materials to your classroom. Purchase inexpensive, self-adhesive address labels and attach one to each of your manuals, trade books, and supplies. Now when someone borrows a resource from you, he will easily see your name and be reminded to return the item when he's finished.

Cynthia Spiess—Gr. 1
Land O' Lakes School
Land O' Lakes, WI

Check It Quick

Students love to complete word-find puzzles, but they're time-consuming to check for accuracy. Use this quick-check system and your word-find puzzles will no longer be a hassle. Use large graph paper as a grid to design each puzzle. Then color in one answer key. Place a sheet of transparency film over your key and trace around the colored areas with a marker. When students complete their puzzles, ask them to color in the boxes as each word is found. When the puzzles are complete, lay the transparent key over each child's paper and you will easily see if your outline matches the student's colored areas. Store the transparent key with a copy of the puzzle for future years' use.

Deborah Ross—Primary
Wayland Alexander School
Hartford, KY

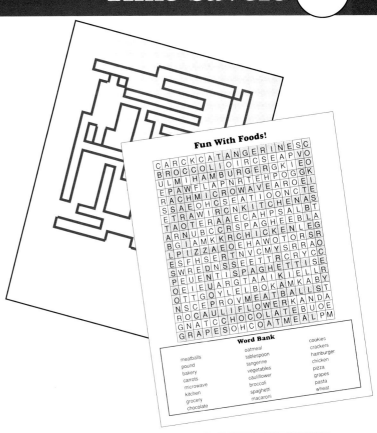

Picture This!

Personalize learning with this unique and charming classroom creation. Early in the year, take a photograph of each child. Cut out and glue each picture to a sturdy circular disk. (The metal ends of frozen juice containers work well.) Magnetize each disk with a piece of magnetic tape, and you instantly have a set of customized classroom manipulatives. Use them for a variety of activities such as showing attendance, recording job assignments, creating graphs, making birthday charts, or as game pieces. The possibilities are endless! Send the magnets home at the end of the year as a memento of the school year.

Therese Hillman—Gr. 3
Burgess Elementary School
Sturbridge, MA

magnetic tape

Stick Pick

Here's an always-at-your-fingertips method for choosing partners, arranging students in line, or organizing teams. Number a class supply of craft sticks and place them number-side-down into a container. When it's time to partner or arrange students, have each child remove a stick from the container. If students are lining up, ask them to arrange themselves in numerical order. To create pairs, call out sets such as "numbers 3 and 16 are partners." If determining teams, group the odd numbers together and the even numbers together. As an alternative, label another set of sticks with the students' names, then choose a stick to select an individual student for errands or prizes.

Therese Hillman—Gr. 3
Burgess Elementary School
Sturbridge, MA

Games Galore

It's no secret that creating file-folder games takes time and energy. Instead of making a separate game for every skill, try making a few generic file-folder gameboards to be used with a variety of skill cards. Use colorful dot stickers to make a path from start to finish on the inside of a file folder, then add other fun stickers for visual interest. Add specific directions to a few of the dots such as "Go back two spaces," or "Move ahead three spaces." Now that the gameboard is complete, use small index cards or shape notepads to program questions for various subjects. The cards should have a question on the front and its answer on the back. Organize the card sets by skill in a shoebox for easy retrieval. To play a game, students just select a set of cards and a gameboard. A student's correct answer is rewarded with one move forward. Students can change games easily by selecting a new set of question cards and keeping the same gameboard.

True Or False? The sun is a star.

START

Move ahead 1 dot.

WOW!

FINISH

GREAT!

GREAT!

Go back 2 dots

Spin again.

Go back 2 dots

GREAT!

SUPER!

Go back 2 dots

How many planets are in our solar system?

Which planet is closest to the sun?

Jeannie Hinyard—Gr. 2
Welder Elementary School
Sinton, TX

Name Check

You'll never have another nameless paper again with this idea. Prior to collecting students' assignments say, "If your name is on your paper, place a check beside it." After students are familiar with the procedure, shorten the reminder to "Name check!" Students will enjoy this opportunity to check part of their papers, and you'll appreciate no more nameless papers!

Jessie ✓

My favorite book is Mr. Popper's Penguins by Richard Atwater. It is a very funny story about a penguin, Captain Cook, that comes to live with Mr. Popper and his family. Soon they have lots of penguins and lots of adventures.

Musical Cleanup

Need an idea for shortening desk cleanup time? Try playing a record or tape for about three to five minutes. Challenge your students to see if they can all finish before the music stops, working so quietly they can hear the music as they work. The result will be a room of clean desks, and that will be music to your ears!

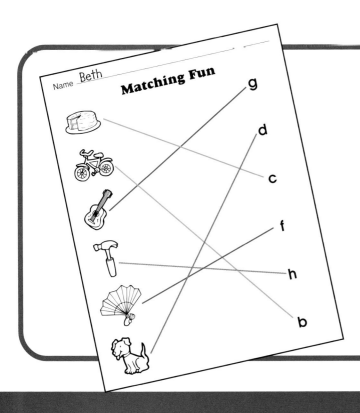

Connect It In Color

Here's a great way to save time correcting matching worksheets. When a worksheet directs students to "draw lines to connect," have your students draw each line with a different color of crayon. The lines will be much easier to follow when it's time to correct, and students will enjoy the colorful addition to the assignment!

Tiny Tooth Tote

Ever wonder what to do with those tiny teeth that students lose during school? You probably have the solution right in your own closet. Many new clothing purchases come with a tiny, resealable plastic bag to hold extra buttons. Keep these little bags on hand in your desk drawer for an occasion such as losing a tooth. Just slip the child's tooth inside the bag for safekeeping. Make the event extraspecial by personalizing the bag and adding a tooth sticker.

Lynda G. Pitcher—Substitute Teacher
Central Dauphin School District
Harrisburg, PA

A Bucketful Of Ideas

The learning possibilities will overflow when you put plastic beach pails to use in your classroom. Purchase a class supply of inexpensive plastic beach pails. On the first day of school, send a pail home with each student and ask her to fill it with a reminder of her summer vacation. Then have students return them to school for a special show-and-tell. Later, use the buckets during a study of rocks. Ask each student to collect an assortment of rocks to investigate and research. The pails also come in handy for storing unearthed fossils in a pretend fossil hunt. For one unit after another, students will enjoy helping you discover a use for the pails.

Carol I. Smith—Grs. 3–4
Westland Academy
Fredericksburg, VA

Portfolio Storage Solution

Many student-made projects, books, art samples, and assessments can add up to more than one folder can hold when creating a child's portfolio. Create the perfect storage for students' work by using discarded cereal boxes. Have each child cover, personalize, and decorate a box. Then store the boxes—with the students' names visible—on a shelf for easy access. Now the work is easy to store and retrieve.

Brooke A. Bock—Gr. 2
Lincoln Elementary
Tyrone, PA

Learning Center Storage

Keep track of cards, game pieces, and gameboards that belong to your learning center games by using this simple storage trick. Use sturdy gift bags (which come in a variety of sizes) to neatly store each game and its accessories. The bags are functional as well as colorful, and the handles make it easy for little hands to carry.

Laurie Schwartz—Substitute
Jamesville, NY

Flash Card Keepers

Are your students always losing flash cards in their desks? Try this simple storage idea and they will always be able to locate their cards. Save a class supply of mini cereal boxes and give one to each student. The boxes are small and easy to store in a desk or school supply box and are the perfect size for storing flash cards. No more missing cards!

Pat Biancardi—Gr. 2
Homan Elementary School
Schererville, IN

Park Pencils Here

Have every student make one of these useful pencil keepers for his desk. All that's needed is a washed, 16-ounce vegetable or soup can for each student. Have each child sponge-paint his can, then add his name. Each pencil holder can be kept in a student's desk, or adorn his desktop. Either way, his pencils will be organized and handy.

Cathi Franz—Grs. 1–3
Edu-Prize School
Gilbert, AZ

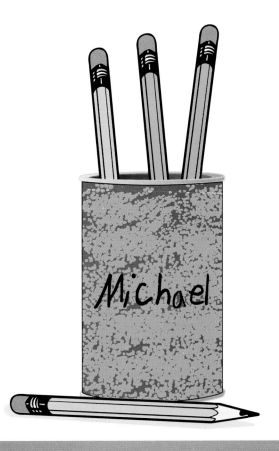

Battleship® Grids

This recycling tip will result in a student-pleasing lesson about coordinates. Use the numbered, blue grid from an unusable Battleship® gameboard as a transparency for your overhead projector (after removing it from the plastic case). The grid is clearly marked and easy to read. Also create a reproducible with a similar grid, and give one to each student for working at his desk. During your lesson, place a marker on the grid (while on the overhead projector) and have students identify the coordinates. Then have students find the same coordinate on their personal grids and mark or color that location. Students' skills at finding coordinates will certainly stay afloat when you put this idea to use!

Liesl Collins—Gr. 3
Littleton Elementary School
Cashion, AZ

Old Mug, New Use

A coffee mug is a common gift, and you probably have several sitting around unused. Turn those dust collectors into useful additions to your classroom by putting a cheerful plant in each mug. Set the mugs on your windowsill, and your colorful mugs can be enjoyed again and again.

Kathleen Geddes Darby—Gr. 1
Community School
Cumberland, RI

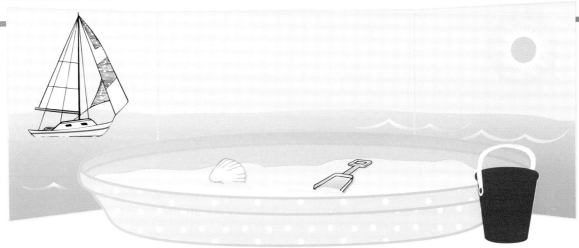

Wading Pool Environments

An inexpensive, plastic wading pool can become a wonderful learning environment in your classroom. Before school begins, purchase a plastic pool, fill it with sand, and put it in your classroom. Display a pail, a shovel, and shells on the sand; then add a three-fold display board behind the pool to show the ocean, a sailboat, and the sun. This attractive setting is a great way to begin a study of the ocean. This is only one way to use the pool throughout the year, but several other displays can be set up as well. You can create a desert scene with cacti and desert animals, or exchange the sand for water to create a living pond for a pond-life study. Just add some lily pads and turtles. The possibilities for this simple summer toy only end with your imagination.

Lisa Tanner—Gr. 3, Summerville Catholic School, Summerville, SC

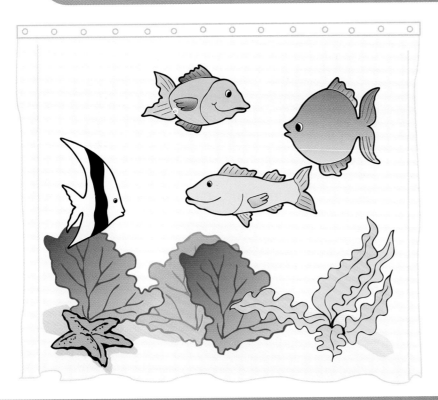

Decorative Liners

When setting the stage for an ocean unit, hang a colorful shower curtain containing a lively ocean scene. Children will love the colorful mood-setting effect. Try using a variety of shower curtain liners that correspond to other units as well. There's no end to the selection or the smiles.

Cindy Ward—Grs. 1–4
Learning Disabilities Teacher
Yellow Branch Elementary
Rustburg, VA

Student Dry-Erase Boards

Make these inexpensive dry-erase boards for students' use in your classroom. You need a sheet of white, glossy bathroom paneling from a home improvement center and electrical tape. Ask to have the paneling cut into 9" x 12" pieces; then finish the edges by applying colorful electrical tape. Voila! You have made instant dry-erase boards to use for student writing, spelling, or math practice. Just distribute some dry-erase markers and let the writing begin!

Wendy Zoch—Gr. 3
Zion Lutheran School
Dallas, TX

Save Those Catalogs

How many school-supply catalogs are stacked up in your classroom during the year? Put this practical tip to use and recycle those outdated versions. A variety of skills can be practiced using the catalogs' pages. Open a catalog and have students print beginning sounds on the pictures using markers. Cut pictures from the catalogs and have students refer to them as story starters for a writing assignment. Cut pictures to use in writing rebus stories, or have students sequence pictures cut from the catalog. The uses are many if you put your imagination to work.

Mary Kay Gallagher—Gr. 1
Seton Catholic School
Moline, IL

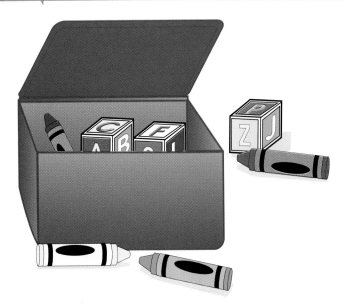

Recycled Storage Boxes

Need handy, stackable storage boxes for your classroom? Try using baby wipe boxes. Their size is perfect for storing a multitude of manipulatives as well as supplies such as bulletin-board letters, paper clips, rubber bands, crayons, and markers. They snap shut (so no spilled contents) and stack neatly on your shelves. You couldn't ask for a better, more inexpensive way to get organized.

Linda Mates—Gr. 2
Public School 206
Brooklyn, NY

From A Box To A Desk

Children will love using these portable desks when working on assignments or projects around your classroom. Use a box with a removable lid (the type copier paper comes in). Secure the lid to the bottom of the box with glue, then cut leg openings in the box as shown. Finish the project by adding a decorative border around the lid's edge. Now students have a hard surface to work on, but don't have to stay in their desks at all times.

Mary Kay Gallagher—Gr. 1
Seton Catholic School
Moline, IL

from this...

to this!

Crayon Caddy

Ask parents to save small metal bandage boxes to reuse in your classroom. When a student's cardboard crayon box begins to sag and soften, give him a bandage tin to use. This sturdy box makes a perfect replacement for worn-out crayon boxes.

Pat Biancardi—Gr. 2
Homan Elementary School
Schererville, IN

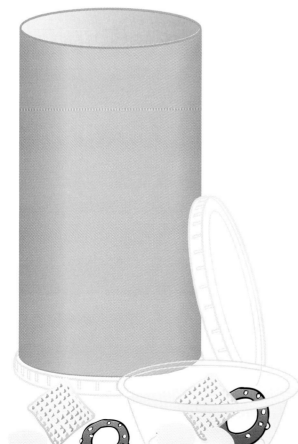

No End To The Uses

Here's a recycling tip that makes use of all parts of a Crystal Light® container. Use the outer canister for storing pushpins, paper clips, game pieces, and other small items. The lids come in a variety of colors so even young children can recognize the contents by the color of the container's lid. Reuse the inner plastic portion cups for counting or sorting math manipulatives, for holding paint, or for distributing snacks. The uses for these versatile containers are endless.

Linda Mates—Gr. 2
Public School 206
Brooklyn, NY

Check It Out!

For a little something extra when making a bulletin-board display, create this distinctive checkerboard background. To produce the background, cover your board with alternating pieces of construction paper in a checkerboard fashion. Top with student work, seasonal cut-outs, or an informative poster to make a striking display. Experiment with different color combinations for holiday arrangements, or try overlapping the pieces of paper for unusual geometric designs. Bulletin-board backgrounds need never be boring again!

Leslie Poythress—Gr. 3
Gray Elementary School
Gray, GA

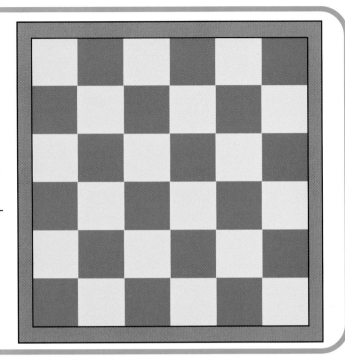

Wallpaper Wonders

For great bulletin-board materials at a minimal cost, look for wallpaper bargains! Many stores have a bin of discontinued wallpaper rolls that can be used as background paper for bulletin-board displays. Look for patterns that correlate with your thematic units. For extra flair, add coordinating wallpaper borders to put the finishing touch on your display. The results? An attractive display that will have co-workers asking, "Who is your interior decorator?"

Mary Kennedy, Royal Valley Elementary School, Hoyt, KS

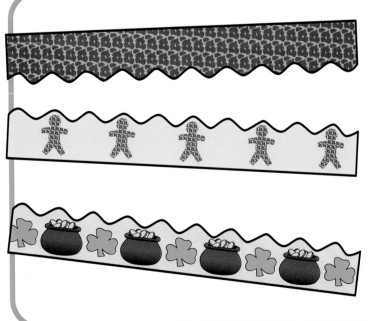

Terrific Trim

Bulletin-board trim can be tailored for any display with this clever idea. Use an old piece of scalloped trim as a pattern for making new border strips. Trace the old border on pieces of tagboard; then decorate the new trim to fit the theme of your display. Attractive borders can be made with sponge-painted shapes, seasonal stickers, or stamp-pad art. Students can work on the border as well, making the display a class-created project. The end product will be a one-of-a-kind border that is custom-made for your classroom.

Rosemary Linden, Royal Valley Elementary School
Hoyt, KS

Caption Connection

Bulletin-board titles are a snap to display with this clever caption idea. When creating a title for your bulletin board, write the letters in an overlapping fashion as shown in the example. Trace around each letter with a dark colored marker so that individual letters stand out. Or, if using die-cut letters, outline each letter with a dark colored marker, then glue the letters together so that whole words are connected. Not only will you save time when adding the title to your display, you'll also put an end to the little worries of spacing problems, keeping letters straight, and storing those loose letters after the display is taken down.

Karen Fouberg—Gr. 3
Mt. Vernon School 17-3
Mt. Vernon, SD

Fancy Letters

Add some panache to any display with this quick and inexpensive way to fancify bulletin-board lettering. After cutting out letters from construction paper, decorate each letter with ministickers, foil stars, or confetti cutouts. Add a seasonal touch to holiday displays by gluing festive confetti shapes on the lettering. Or reinforce an informative bulletin-board topic using thematic chart stickers to decorate the title. If desired, laminate the decorated letters for durability. With minimal effort and expense, you have added that extra touch that turns a bulletin board into an eye-catching display.

Debra Dahl—Gr. 2
St. Charles Primary
Chippewa Falls, WI

Fabulous Fabric

This bulletin-board tip is not only a time-saver for you, it's also an earth-friendly, paper-saving idea! Instead of using background paper on your bulletin-board displays, try using a fabric covering. Measure the size of your bulletin board, then purchase the necessary amount of fabric and hem it around the edges. The fabric won't fade, is washable, is easy to store, and can be used for years to come. When it's time to create a new bulletin-board display, you won't have to head for the supply closet and wrestle with bulky background paper. A fabric covering will make an easy-on-the-eye, easy-to-use, and easy-on-the environment bulletin-board background.

Tina M. Miller—Gr. 1
St. Mary's Catholic School
Wilmington, NC

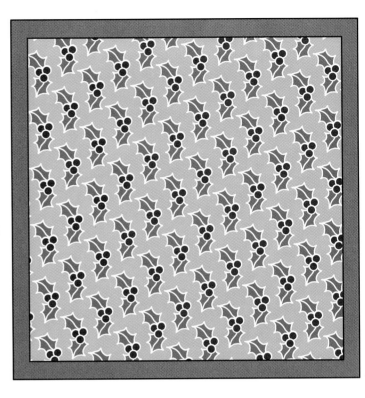

"Tree-mendous" 3-D Displays

This 3-D display idea is guaranteed to make any bulletin board stand out ! To create a 3-D tree cutout, fold a 12' x 18" piece of brown construction paper in half lengthways. Trace half of a symmetrical tree outline onto the paper as shown. Cut out the resulting tree shape and trace it onto a second piece of construction paper, repeating the process to produce an identical tree shape. Place the trees together so that the fold lines match up. Apply a thin line of glue along the fold lines, then press together firmly. When it's dry, mount the tree to the bulletin board by stapling two sides of the cutout to the board. Complete the display with student-created seasonal poems and stories and written on leaf shapes. The result will be a "tree-mendous" exhibit!

adapted from an idea by
Rita Arnold, Grs. K–5, Special Education
Alden Hebron Grade School, Hebron, IL

Welcome a new crop of students with this home-grown greeting. Cover a bulletin board with green background paper; then add a strip of blue paper along the top to create a sky. Next use a sponge dipped in brown tempera paint to make rows for a garden plot. While the paint is drying, use the pattern on page 150 to duplicate a class set of carrots on orange construction paper. Write the name of a student on a carrot; then "plant" it in the garden by making a small slit into the background paper and sliding the carrot into place. Top off each carrot with a green crepe-paper stem, and your bulletin board is ready for a brand-new year!

Kim Clasquin—Gr. 1, St. Paul Elementary School, Highland, IL

This sunny exhibit will brighten up a bulletin board as well as promote students' self-esteem. To create the display, cover a bulletin board with a blue background. Mount a large yellow sun-shaped cutout to the center of the board. Arrange student photographs inside the sun shape and add a title proclaiming, "What A Bright Bunch Of Students!" Your students' faces will be equally as bright when they see themselves featured in the display!

Beth Fondale—Gr. 2
St. Rose School, New Lexington, OH

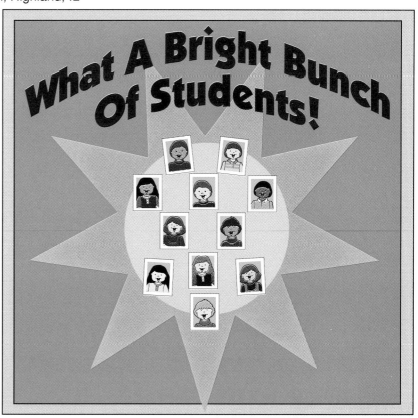

Send a bushel of greetings to your new students with this 3-D bulletin board. Cover a bulletin board with white paper and add a dark green border. To create the 3-D effect, obtain a fruit basket from a supermarket or produce stand. Cut the basket in half and mount it to the bulletin board. Use the pattern on page 150 to duplicate a class supply of apples on colored construction paper. Program each apple with the name of a student. Add the catchy title to let your children know that you are looking forward to a new year.

Phyllis Bowling—Gr. 2, Smithville Elementary, Smithville, MS

Student smiles and fall colors provide seasonal style to this autumn bulletin-board idea! To create the display, take a picture of each student. Then use the pattern on page 151 to duplicate a class set of acorns on brown construction paper. Mount each student's photo atop an acorn cutout and attach it to the bulletin board. Enlarge the frisky squirrel character on page 151 and add it to the display. What a "class-y" way to welcome fall!

Leslie Voorhees—Gr. 1, Ashley Grade School, Ashley, IL

Let your students know what lies ahead in the new school year with a bulletin board that inspires them to explore their new grade level. Use a map as background paper to cover a bulletin board. Then add actual items used in your grade level. Use colored paper to duplicate a class supply of the car pattern on page 152, and write the name of a student on each car cutout. Place the cars around the display to create a border that conveys traveling through a new school year. Add a title such as "Let's Explore A New Grade!" and you're ready to roll!

Marsha Basanda—Gr. 3, Bryson Elementary, Simpsonville, SC

This "season premiere" bulletin board will receive high ratings as you tune in to a new school year. Sketch a television cabinet on the poster board, color it, and cut it out, leaving a hole where the screen would be. Attach white paper to the back of the cutout to create the screen. Add pipe cleaners or a wire hanger to the top to resemble an antenna. Mount the resulting TV set on the bulletin board as shown. On the first day of school, have each student draw a self-portrait. Arrange the portraits on the TV screen in a collage fashion. Now pass the popcorn and let the show begin!

Sarah Mertz—Grs. 1–2, Owenton, KY

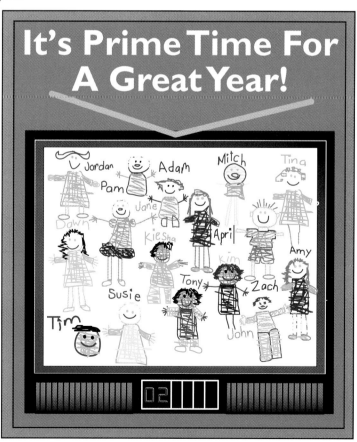

Broadcast the news of good behavior with this bulletin board that reinforces classroom rules. Distribute a copy of the television pattern on page 153 to each child. Instruct each student to illustrate the television screen with a picture of himself modeling good behavior. Then have the student write a caption under the picture to describe the classroom rule he is following. Have students color the remainder of the pattern to resemble a TV set. Now that's a performance with star quality!

Nori R. Cortez—Gr. 2, Anthon Elementary, Uvalde, TX

Who is the teacher's pet? Show your students who holds that title with a bulletin board featuring pets of the fur, feather, and fin persuasion. To create the display, ask your fellow staff members to supply photographs of their pets. Arrange the photos on a bulletin board along with a nametag or picture of each pet's owner. Add a caption announcing, "Look At The Teachers' Pets!" Everyone is sure to enjoy the resulting pictorial pet parade.

Diann Hardesty—Gr. 1, McKinley School, Toledo, OH

Get your classroom helpers off on the right note with this hip-hoppin' display of job assignments. Enlarge the jukebox pattern on page 154 and mount it in the center of the bulletin board. Write the name of each classroom job on a sentence strip, and place the strips around the jukebox pattern. Then construct a record for each student by tracing a six-inch circle on black paper. Add a small, yellow circle to the center of each record cutout and program with the name of a student. To assign the classroom duties, pin a record cutout under each job title. Your students will be right in tune with their job assignments!

Lauren Egizio—Substitute Teacher, Easton Public Schools, Easton, MA

There's nothing fishy about this colorful display of student artwork. To prepare, duplicate a class set of the fish pattern on page 155. Have students decorate their fish with watercolors, crayons, or markers. Attach the fish to a blue background and add the title "We're Swimming Towards Success!" Embellish with seaweed and shell cutouts along the bottom. What a "fin-tastic" display!

Andrea Hunter—Gr. 1, Fullington Academy, Pinehurst, GA

Show your students how worthy they are with this funny-money display! To create the bulletin board, you will need a picture of each student and a class supply of the dollar bill pattern on page 152. Cut out a circle shape around each student's face from the photograph and glue it to the center of the dollar pattern. Watch the delight on student faces when they see the value you have attached to them!

Cindy Ward—Grs. 1–4, Learning Disabilities Teacher, Yellow Branch Elementary School, Rustburg, VA

Encourage students to go bananas over books with this bulletin board that tracks reading progress. Enlarge the monkey pattern on page 156. Mount it on the bulletin board along with a banana tree fashioned from brown and green corrugated paper. Attach a large pocket in the shape of a basket to hold banana cutouts made from the pattern on page 156. As each student reads a book, he writes the title, the author, and his name on a banana and attaches it to the tree. As the tree becomes heavy with bananas, you'll know your students have gone ape over reading!

Sr. Maribeth Theis—Gr. 2
Mary Of Lourdes Elementary School
Little Falls, MN

Add some sparkle to a display of student work with this gem of a design. To create the display, cover a bulletin board with an aluminum foil background. Distribute a copy of the ring pattern on page 155 to each student and have him color it using a gem-tone crayon. Drizzle the colored pattern with glue, then sprinkle with glitter. Allow to dry, then cut the rings out and mount them on the board to top off an example of each student's brightest work!

Sarah Mertz—Grs. 1–2, Owenton, KY

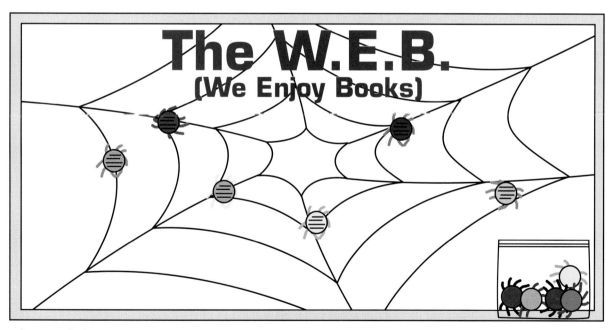

Spin an interest in literature with this cumulative display of classroom favorites. Cover a bulletin board with white paper. Use heavy black yarn and stick pins to create a web design on the background. Then make a supply of spiders by cutting a thin sheet of Styrofoam® into two-inch circles. Cover each circle with tissue paper and insert eight short pieces of pipe cleaner into the circle to resemble legs. Each time a book is shared with the class, use a permanent marker to write the title and author on a spider. Attach it to the web. As the web becomes crowded with crawling creatures, you'll know your students have snagged an interest in books!

Sr. Maribeth Theis—Gr. 2, Mary Of Lourdes Elementary School, Little Falls, MN

This activity yields two great results—an attractive student-made bulletin board and practice in class teamwork. Arrange students in groups of four. Have each group brainstorm ways they are alike and different. Record their responses on chart paper. Distribute a copy of the pattern on page 157 to each student. Provide art supplies for the groups to use as they decorate their patterns to resemble themselves. Then mount the resulting "people" on a bulletin board along with the charted responses from the brainstorming session. Students will be proud to see their group efforts displayed in this teamwork arrangement.

Kristen McLaughlin—Gr. 1, Daniel Boone Area School District, Boyertown, PA

Your students will smile from ear to ear as they help fashion this cheery display. Gather a supply of world maps and a snapshot of each student; then set to work to create the display. Distribute a map to each student and instruct him to cut a six-inch circle from it. Then have him glue his picture in the center of the circle. Arrange the circles on a bulletin board with the title "We All Smile In The Same Language." Now show us those pearly whites!

Angela Hopkins—Grs. K–6 Spanish Teacher, St. Cecilia Catholic School, Clare, MI

Help your students to spread warm feelings on Teacher Appreciation Day with a display to honor all the teachers in your school. Assign each student the name of a teacher on campus. Then, have the student make a card for the teacher. Provide a time for each student to deliver the card personally. When he returns to the classroom, the student draws a picture of his assigned teacher. Display the finished portraits on a prominent bulletin board or in the hallway for all to see and enjoy. Won't your co-workers be surprised?

Deborah Ross—Primary Teacher, Wayland Alexander School, Hartford, KY

Boost geography skills and pique an interest in other countries and cultures with a bulletin board that stays up year-round. Mount a world map and add the caption "Where In The World Is _____ ?" Each week fill in the blank with the name of a country written on a sentence strip. Students study the map for the location of the country, but do not reveal its whereabouts once they have found it. Encourage the students to look for newspaper articles, books, and other information about the featured country. At the end of the week, have students share any information they have collected about the country. By the end of the year, your students will feel like world travelers!

Laurie Gibbons—Gr. 1, Elm Street Elementary, Newnan, GA

Still-Life Designs

This still-life project uses teamwork to generate artwork. Divide your students into several small groups, and provide each group with a collection of objects. The collection could include seasonal items such as autumn leaves and nuts, holly berries and pinecones, or spring flowers in a basket. Invite each group to arrange its objects into an attractive display. Then instruct the group members to sit around the display at different angles to sketch the still-life arrangement. Display each group's finished projects together to provide students with the opportunity to see the arrangement from different perspectives.

Joann Bollinger—Gr. 3
Plains Elementary School
Timberville, VA

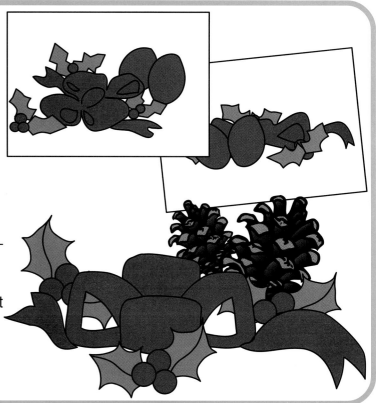

Fingerprint Flowerpot

Students work together to create this fabulous flowerpot that can be used as a gift for a student teacher, room mother, or classroom helper. Provide a large clay pot and a black permanent marker, and instruct each student to write his name on the brim of the pot. Decorate the rest of the pot with colorful fingerprint flowers. Place a shallow container of yellow tempera paint by the pot and instruct each student to dip his thumb into the paint, then create a flower-petal design on the flowerpot with his thumbprints. The student then dips his pinkie into a second color of paint and presses his fingerprint in the center of the flower. If desired, use a green permanent marker to draw stems and leaves. Line the flowerpot with tissue paper and fill it with thank-you notes, wrapped candies, or a small plant. What a lovely gift from the entire class!

Leigh Anne Newsom
E. W. Chittum Elementary
Chesapeake, VA

Spiffy Snowman Pin

Recycling is the key to creating these festive pins for holiday giftgiving. To construct a pin, each student will need a white Styrofoam® packing peanut, an acorn cap, and a piece of red yarn. Provide a supply of fine-tipped markers for students to create a face and a row of buttons on the peanut as shown. Help students glue the acorn cap atop the snowman's head for a little hat and then tie the yarn around the center of the peanut to resemble a scarf. Attach a pinback to the completed project, and the snowman is ready to greet the holiday season.

Leigh Anne Newsom
E. W. Chittum Elementary
Chesapeake, VA

Easy Ice-Cream Ornaments

These ice-cream ornaments add a tasty touch to holiday decorating. To create the decoration, each student will need a ball-shaped ornament with a hook attachment, an ice-cream cone, glue, and glitter. Apply a line of glue around the rim of the cone; then place the ornament on top as shown. Drizzle a few drops of glue from the ornament and sprinkle with glitter. Allow approximately 30 minutes for drying time; then these delicious decorations are ready to be put on display.

Leigh Anne Newsom

Seasonal Windsock

As the seasons change, try an art project to reinforce the characteristics of the season and provide an attractive touch to your classroom decor. Provide each student with a 12" x 18" piece of construction paper and have him write the name of the season on it. If desired, illustrations or seasonal cutouts can be added to the paper. Show the students how to roll the paper into a cylinder, and help them staple or glue the ends together. Next distribute several 3" x 18" strips of craft paper in seasonal colors to each student. Instruct the student to write a word or sentence about the current season on each strip. Glue the strips to the bottom of the cylinder to resemble streamers. Use a hole puncher and a length of yarn to attach a handle to each windsock. Suspend the windsocks from the ceiling to celebrate the arrival of a brand-new time of year.

adapted from an idea by Kelly Carrier—Gr. 1
Clarkmoor Elementary
Sumner, WA

Marvelous Mandala

Individuality shines through on these unique mandala projects. Provide each student with a white, eight-inch paper circle. Instruct the student to draw a picture of something very important to him in the center of the circle. Around the picture he is to draw a circular pattern using an illustration that reflects something significant in his life. The student continues adding circular rows of pictures that have special meaning to him. Mount the completed mandalas on colored construction paper and display them in a prominent place in the classroom. Each finished project tells a story about its creator and reminds us how important it is to be a unique individual.

Jacquie Nielson—Substitute Teacher
Vancouver, British Columbia
Canada

Stained-Glass Creations

These stained-glass apples add a colorful touch to your classroom windows. To make the project, provide each student with a copy of the apple pattern on page 150, a 9" x 12" piece of red construction paper, and a square of colored cellophane. Instruct the student to use the apple pattern to trace two shapes onto the construction paper. Cut out the resulting shapes; then fold each in half. Place one cutout inside the other so that the folds are together; then cut out the center section of the apples, leaving a 1/2-inch border around the outside of each cutout. Unfold the shapes. Place a square of colored cellophane in between the apple cutouts and glue it into place. Trim the excess cellophane from the edges. Display the finished projects in your sunniest window and watch the colors light up your classroom.

Jane Oliva—Gr. 2
St. Robert Bellermine School
Bayside, NY

Creative Candleholders

Add a glow to any season with these easy-to-make holiday lights. To construct a holiday candleholder, each student will need an empty 2-liter soda bottle, a 12-inch square of fabric, and a length of matching ribbon. Assist each child in cutting off the top one-fourth of the soda bottle. (The bottom of the bottle may be saved for a later use.) Turn the fabric square right-side down and place the bottle top on it. Gather the corners of the fabric and fold over the bottle top, securing the fabric at the neck with a rubber band. Tie the ribbon over the rubber band. The opening at the top of the bottle is just the right size to hold a taper candle. What a nice centerpiece or holiday gift for your students to take home!

Michelle Jagitsch—Gr. 3
Odell Elementary
Odell, IL

Musical Inspirations

Combine music appreciation with an art activity to inspire some very creative drawings. Play a recording of a genre of music that your children might not be familiar with, such as jazz, opera, or blues. Have the students listen to the recording with their eyes closed, and ask them to visualize images in the music. Then distribute a piece of drawing paper to each student and play the recording a second time. Instruct students to draw the images they "see" in the music. Encourage students to use colors that match the tone of the music. Provide a time for each student to share her drawing with the class, explaining how the music inspired her drawing.

Kathleen Guide—Gr. 3
St. Ann's School
Raritan, NJ

These are the feelings we get from jazz music.

Chanda

Tim

Derek

Kim

High-Flying Display

Get ready for windy weather with a display of colorful kites. Create kite-shaped templates from poster board; then place them in a center with a supply of gift wrap, yarn, and fabric scraps. Each student uses the template to trace the kite shape on two pieces of wrapping paper. Arrange the resulting shapes so that the print side shows on the front and the back of the kite. Place a template and a length of string between the cutouts, then glue them together. For an added touch, tie scraps of fabric to the tail of the kite. When they're dry, suspend the kites from the ceiling for a bright and breezy decor.

Leigh Anne Newsom
E. W. Chittum Elementary
Chesapeake, VA

How Puzzling!

Create a distinctive gift for anyone who has helped the pieces fall into place during the school year. Have students use pieces from a jigsaw puzzle to create pins to present as thank-you gifts or tokens of appreciation. Distribute five or six pieces to each student and instruct him to glue the pieces into an overlapping arrangement. Use a hot glue gun to affix a pin backing to the back of the arrangement. Attach the completed pin to a piece of poster board bearing the message "Thanks for giving us a piece of your time!" This pin is a nice token for anyone who has offered his time and energy in your classroom, or can be adapted for a Mother's Day gift.

Leigh Anne Newsom, E. W. Chittum Elementary, Chesapeake, VA

Thanks for giving us a piece of your time!

Art Appreciation

Lead a classwide show of appreciation by having your students make these mini chalkboard magnets for Teacher Appreciation Day. To make a magnet, each student will need a two-inch square, black ceramic tile. Provide a paint pen for the student to use to write a message such as "Teachers Are Special" or "A+ Teacher." If desired, place a small apple sticker under the message. Then attach a strip of magnetic tape to the back of each tile. When Teacher Appreciation Day arrives, have students hand deliver a magnet to each teacher on campus. What teacher wouldn't be pleased with such a useful and attractive gift?

Deborah Ross—Primary Teacher, Wayland Alexander School, Hartford, KY

Flowerpot Photos

Give the gift of a smiling face with this floral frame project. Gather a photo of each student, several sheets of poster board, and a class supply of miniature clay pots, craft sticks, and Styrofoam®. Instruct each student to cut two flower shapes from the poster board, making them large enough for his photo to show through the center of the flower. Cut a circle from the center of one flower and glue the photo to the back. Place the remaining flower cutout behind the photo, insert the craft stick between the flower shapes, and then glue in place. When it's dry, stand the flower inside the flowerpot, using a piece of Styrofoam® to hold it in place. Then add green crinkled gift-wrap stuffing on top of the Styrofoam®. The completed project can be presented as a gift for any occasion. What beautiful blossoms you've cultivated!

Leigh Anne Newsom

Arts And Crafts

Super Stencil

Make the most of materials you already have on hand for this super stencil idea. Create a set of stencils with a shape puncher and several strips of tagboard. Punch a row of shapes into each tagboard strip and place in a center with an ink stamp pad, a few makeup sponge wedges, and a supply of paper. Students visit the center to create prints by inking the sponge and rubbing over the stencil onto a sheet of paper. Use a variety of stencil shapes for activities such as making birthday cards, creating holiday gift wrap, and experimenting with patterns. What a great activity at such a minimal cost!

Carla Voegele—Grs. K–4, Pearl Creek Colony School, Iroquois, SD

Well-Versed Drawings

Incorporate art with a poetry unit to maximize student creativity. Distribute a piece of white construction paper to each student and instruct him to fold it into four sections. Then read aloud several selections of poetry to the class. Have each student choose four of the poems to illustrate, using a section on the construction paper for each drawing. Read the poems a second time, providing time for students to work on their drawings after each poem. When the drawings are complete, allow students to share their illustrations with the class. Discuss the similarities and differences in the responses to the same poem. What a "verse-atile" way to encourage creative thinking!

Nancy Lujan—Gr. 3, C. I. Waggoner Elementary, Tempe, AZ

Bigmouthed Puppet

Create something to talk about with this bigmouthed puppet pattern. To make this chatty character, distribute two 9-inch paper plates to each student. Instruct the student to fold each paper plate in half and cut one of the plates into two pieces. Staple or glue a half-plate section to the top of the folded plate, leaving the straight edge open (this is where the student will put his hand to operate the puppet's mouth). Repeat the step to attach the other half-plate section to the bottom of the folded plate. Draw a face on top of the stapled plates, and color the inside section to resemble a mouth. Have the student slip his hand into the puppet for a discussion of dental health, nutritious snacks, or lunchroom manners. Or have each student create a character for a classroom play. The results will speak for themselves!

Marsha Weiner—Gr. 2, Churchill School, Homewood, IL

What An Attractive Gift!

Here's a gift-giving idea that can be adapted to fit any occasion. Visit a local hardware store to purchase a class supply of two-inch ceramic floor tiles and a roll of magnetic tape. Then provide each student with one tile and an assortment of fine-tipped permanent markers and small seasonal stickers. Instruct each student to write his name or holiday greeting on his tile, then embellish it with stickers or drawings. Add a strip of magnetic tape to the back of each tile. The result is a simple and inexpensive project that makes a useful gift for family or friends.

Deborah Ross—Primary Teacher
Wayland Alexander School
Hartford, KY

Compliment Wheels

Let someone know how special they are with this wheel of good tidings. To make a compliment wheel, each student will need a paper plate, a piece of construction paper, and a brad. Instruct the student to trace the plate onto the construction paper, then cut out the resulting circle. Cut a pie-shaped wedge from the plate, then use a pencil to divide the construction-paper circle into sections approximately the same size as the wedge. In each section, draw or write a reason why a special someone is important to you. When each section is complete, place the paper plate atop the circle and fasten together with a brad. Decorate the front of the plate with a message such as "You Are Special Because..." The recipient turns the plate to reveal the messages of gratitude from the sender. What a wonderful way to keep good thoughts circulating!

Leigh Anne Newsom
E. W. Chittum Elementary
Chesapeake, VA

Snazzy Pen Project

This craft project can be used as a gift-giving idea, but students might not want to part with the finished project! To create these unusual pens, each student will need a disposable ink pen and assorted colors of baking clay. Assist the student in removing the ink cartridge and cap from the pen; then collect them for safekeeping, as they will be reinserted at a later stage. Instruct each student to work a small amount of clay in his hands to make it pliable, then mold it around the empty pen cylinder. Encourage students to be creative by adding several colors or raised designs as they cover the pens with the clay. (Caution students not to cover the opening for the ink cartridge!) Place the pens on a cookie sheet and bake in a preheated oven according to the directions on the package of clay. Remove them from the oven and allow to cool; then replace the ink cartridges. The result will be unique pens for any gift-giving occasion!

Cynthia Spiess—Gr. 1, Land O' Lakes Elementary
Land O' Lakes, WI

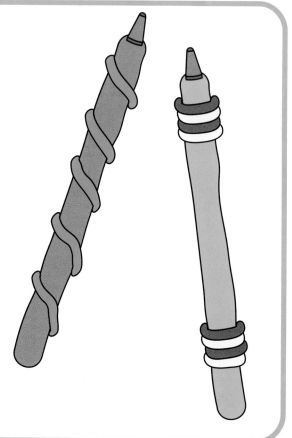

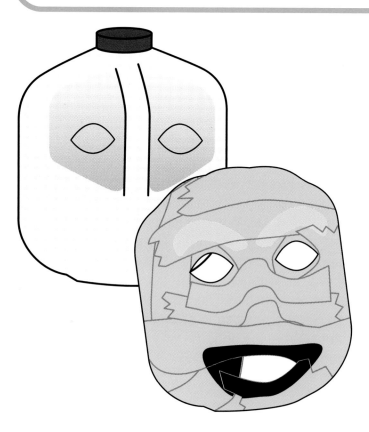

Milk-Jug Masks

A plastic milk jug and some papier-mâché mix makes this mask-making project as easy as can be! To make a papier-mâché mask, each student will need a gallon-size jug cut in half lengthwise with the handle piece attached. The handle of the jug makes an excellent form for the nose piece. Provide a permanent marker for each student to use to sketch a place for the eyeholes on the jug. Have her apply the strips of papier-mâché to the jug to create the mask, making sure to leave the eyeholes uncovered. When the material is dry, peel it away from the plastic jug. Then get out the paints and watch as your students create some very unusual faces!

Mary Kay Gallagher—Gr. 1, Seton Catholic School
Moline, IL

Art Center Organizer

Keep your art center clutter-free with this handy organizing tip. Purchase a see-through multipocket shoe bag and fill each pocket with a material to be used at the center. Label each pocket with the name of the object inside. Students will be able to locate any item they need by glancing at the labeled pocket, and can return materials to the proper place during cleanup time. And because the organizer is see-through, you can see when supplies need to be replenished. Now there's a way to make your art center hassle-free!

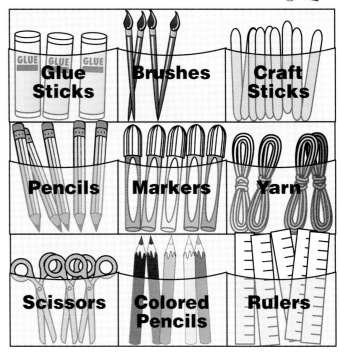

Tablecloth Time-Saver

Does it take longer to clean up after an art project than it took to create it? Cut down on cleanup time by covering desks or tables with a vinyl tablecloth before embarking on an art activity. The flannel backing helps the cloth to stay in place, and unlike newspapers, it can be used again and again. A damp cloth takes care of paint spills or glue drips, then the tablecloth can be stored until it's time for another project. What a nice alternative to scraping paint off desks or gathering up wet newspaper after an art session!

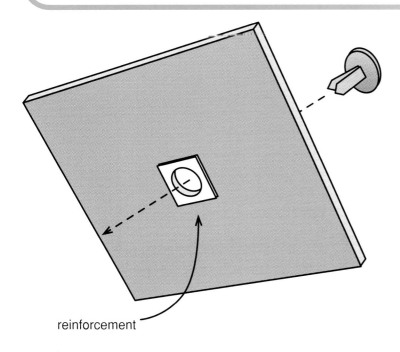

reinforcement

Send In The Reinforcements!

Students love art projects that contain movable pieces, but so often the brad fasteners used to connect the pieces end up tearing the paper instead. A simple remedy to this problem is to apply a self-stick hole reinforcement around the area for the brad. The attached piece can still move freely, but the movement of the brad won't cause the paper to rip or the hole to become too large. Sometimes it's the small things that make a big difference!

Art Recipes

Use the following recipes to cook up some creative projects!

No-Cook Modeling Dough

2 cups flour
1 cup salt
2 tablespoons vegetable oil
water
food coloring (optional)

Mix the ingredients, using enough water to create the desired consistency. The oil in this dough will keep it from hardening. Store the dough in an airtight container after each use.

Baking Dough (Big Batch)

2 cups flour
1 cup salt
 water

Mix enough water with the dry ingredients to make a dough. Create designs by flattening the dough with a rolling pin, then cutting out shapes with cookie cutters or a plastic knife. Bake the dough at 300°F for about an hour. When cooled, the dough can be painted and shellacked.

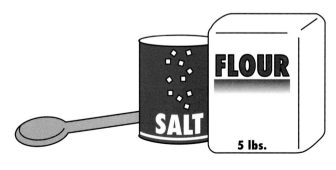

Baking Dough (Individual Amount)

4 tablespoons flour
1 tablespoon salt
2 tablespoons water

Have each student measure and mix the ingredients. Then flatten the dough and shape with a cookie cutter or plastic knife. Bake the dough at 350°F for 1 to 1 1/2 hours. Decorate when cooled.

Homemade Play Dough

1 cup flour
1/2 cup salt
2 teaspoons cream of tartar
1 cup water
1 teaspoon vegetable oil
food coloring (optional)

Mix the dry ingredients together, then add the remaining ingredients and stir. In a heavy skillet, cook the mixture for two or three minutes, stirring frequently. Knead the dough until it becomes soft and smooth. When it's cool, store the dough in an airtight container.

Shiny Paint

1 part white liquid glue
1 part tempera paint

Mix the ingredients. This paint will retain a wet look after it has dried.

Salt Paint

2 teaspoons salt
1 teaspoon liquid starch
a few drops of tempera paint

Mix the ingredients together. The salt gives a frosted appearance to the paint.

Dazzling Tempera Paint

2 cups dry tempera paint
1 cup liquid starch
1 cup liquid soap (clear or white)

Mix the paint and soap; add the starch and stir. If the mixture becomes too thick, add more liquid soap. The result will be a bright-colored paint. Store the paint in a coffee can with a plastic lid.

Easy Papier-Mâché

liquid starch
cold water
newspaper torn into strips

Mix equal parts of liquid starch and cold water. Dip the newspaper strips into the mixture before applying to a form of chicken wire or rolled newspaper.

Pre-Conference Preparations

Increase the productivity of parent conferences with a pre-conference form for parents to fill out at home. A simple but thought-provoking form can include questions such as "What do you think your child's strengths/weaknesses are?", "Do you have concerns about your child's social interaction?", or "What seems to be your child's favorite part of school this year?" By filling out the form ahead of time, parents can reflect on specific areas they wish to discuss, and reduce the chance of having a teacher-driven conference. Parents will appreciate the opportunity to focus on what matters most to them—their child!

Susan Johnson—Gr. 3
Steiner Ranch Elementary
Austin, TX

Child's Name _____ *Ben McFayden*

What do you think your child's strengths/weaknesses are?

Ben loves to read and seems to retain what he reads well. His area of challenge seems to be math, especially word problems.

Do you have concerns about your child's social interaction?

Ben is a little shy, but he seems at ease in interacting with the children in the class. He may need some encouragement though to ask questions in front of the class.

What seems to be your child's favorite part of school this year?

He especially liked the multicultural project and the History reenactments.

Parent's signature _____ *Mrs. Doris McFayden*

My child read
Tuck Everlasting
(name of book)

Mr. Rodney Luck
(parent's signature)

☐ My child read the book.
☑ We took turns reading.
☐ I read the book to my child.

Reading Response Form

Many times a note is sent home for parents to sign when their child completes an at-home reading assignment. Why not use the opportunity to gather more information about a child's reading progress by adding a simple checklist to the signature slip? Under the signature line, add a place for parents to indicate whether the child read with little or no help, took turns reading with the parent, or had the book read to him by the parent. You'll have a better understanding of the reading situation at home without asking the parents to complete a complicated form.

Sherry Geier—Gr. 1
Silver Elementary School
Olney, IL

Book Notes

Encourage young readers to complete reading assignments at home with the help of book notes. Each time an at-home story is assigned, send home a note for parents to sign. The note should include spaces for the parents to fill in the title of the story, the date, and their signature. If a student brings a completed form to school the following day, he places a sticker on his progress chart. When he has earned five stickers, reward him with a small surprise. Students will be eager to attend to their reading homework, and parents will be on the lookout for these assignments.

Peggy Seibel—Gr. 2
St. Mary's School
Ellis, KS

Homework Folder

A homework folder is just the thing to help students become organized at home and at school. Provide a folder for each student in your class, and attach a chart with a square for each week of the school year on the inside cover. Each square should be labeled with the date of the week it represents. Send the folder home each Friday with the graded papers for the week. The parents will have the weekend to review the papers and initial the square on the chart, indicating they have seen the papers for that week. On Monday, place a sticker in the square to show that you have seen the parent's initials. Parents will appreciate the routine, and the chart provides a visual account of the student's responsibility with his folder.

Deb Olson—Grs. K–2, Gates School, Broken Bow, NE

Home And School Connection

Happy Notes

Parents are always eager to hear good news about their children. Ensure that each student has a positive message to take home each grading period with this easy system. At the beginning of each grading period, label an encouraging note or award certificate with each student's name. Divide the notes equally by the number of weeks in the grading period, then clip the notes to the corresponding weeks in your plan book. At the end of each week, simply distribute the notes to the students. With a little effort in advance, you'll be assured that each student will receive a positive note to take home during the grading period.

Sherry Geier—Gr. 1, Silver Elementary School, Olney, IL

Personalized Progress Reports

Progress reports are an essential and informative tool for both parents and teachers, but can sometimes fail to provide an in-depth picture of a student's performance. Add a more personalized touch to these reports by having students write a weekly letter to their parents. The letter should inform parents of current topics of study, weekly test scores, and a conduct evaluation. Send each report home in a special folder that parents will know to look for, and provide a section for parents to write a response back to the child. Keep previous reports in the folder for documentation of goals, recurrent concerns, and evidence of achievement. This progress report system will keep everyone in the know and will result in a journal of the student's year in school.

Deborah Ross—Primary Teacher, Wayland Alexander School, Hartford, KY

Who took lunch count today?

What story did you hear after recess?

What country are you studying this week?

Question Suggestion

Add a special note of interest on your back-to-school supply list—a list of specific questions parents can ask their children about the school day. These questions will give parents an insight to your classroom routines by cluing them in about typical daily happenings. Provide sample questions such as "Who took lunch count today?", "What story did you hear after recess?", or "What country are you studying this week?" Now when parents inquire what happened at school that day, the typical response of, "Oh, nothing" will be replaced with a more detailed version!

Julie Furleigh—Gr. 2, La Salle Avenue School
Los Angeles, CA

Parent Homework

Start out the year with a little homework—for parents! Ask parents to list three goals they hope their child will accomplish in the upcoming year. The goals can be academic, social, athletic, or for personal responsibility. Encourage parents to let this assignment generate a discussion with their child. You may also refer to the goals during parent conferences during the year. Parents will be pleased that you want their input and will appreciate your interest in their child.

Susan Johnson—Gr. 3, Steiner Ranch Elementary, Austin, TX

<u>Homework For Parents</u>

Child's name ___Frankie Foster___
Parent's name ___Gracie Foster___

List three goals you and your child hope to accomplish this year.

We would like to see an accelerated improvement in Frankie's math skills.

We hope that Frankie will continue to excel in reading, writing, and comprehension.

We would like to see Frankie become more comfortable with speaking up in class, giving reports, etc.

Book Bag Bonus

Sending a book home for students to share with their parents is a great way to reinforce reading practice, but after a while, the novelty wears off. Perk up the home-reading assignment with a special book bag that students take home once a month. Decorate a canvas tote and fill it with a book, an activity card, and any materials necessary to complete the activity. Let your book choice pertain to the current season or an upcoming holiday, and choose an activity that correlates to the story. For October, a Halloween book could be accompanied by a simple mask-making project. February's selection could reflect Valentine's Day, President's Month, or Afro-American History Month, teamed up with an activity for a collage or mobile to represent the theme. Send the bag home with a different student every night. At the end of the month, each student has had the opportunity to share the literature activity with his family. At-home reading assignments will be back in demand!

Linda Stroik—Gr. 2, Bannach Elementary, Stevens Point, WI

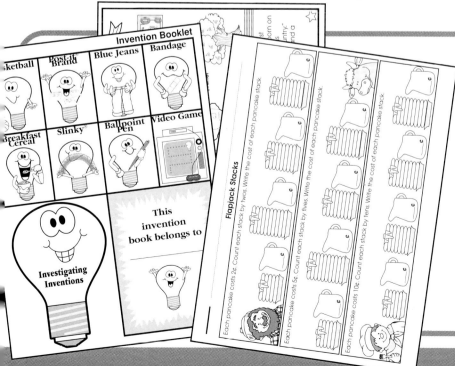

Recycled Reinforcers

Leftover workbooks and extra copies of worksheets need not end up in the trash can—put them to good use! Place them in a box in your classroom for parents to peruse when waiting for a conference or picking up their child after school. The papers are perfect for practicing skills at home or reinforcing a subject when the student needs a little extra help. What an earth-friendy way to promote parent involvement!

Quick and Easy Postcards

Let your computer make home/school communication as easy as can be! At the beginning of the year, print out a supply of address labels for each student in your class. Store the labels with a stack of postcards. When you are ready to send a note home, simply affix a label onto a postcard and jot a short note. A quick glance at your supply of unused labels will remind you how many postcards you have sent to each student. Imagine how thrilled the students will be to find a note at home congratulating them on a test grade or thanking them for positive behavior. What an easy way to brighten someone's day!

Leigh Anne Newsom
E. W. Chittum Elementary School
Chesapeake, VA

Jamie,

I was so impressed with the way you helped Christine out when she fell down. You were a very good friend to her and I'm proud of you.

Your teacher,
Mr. Simpson

Summer Mail

Are you a classroom shutterbug? Then use your photos to help strengthen the home/school connection! When you take pictures of your students during the year, take advantage of the double-print developing offer. Keep one copy of the photo in your classroom scrapbook, and save the other copy for a special summer correspondence. During the summer break, write a short note to each of your former students and enclose a few pictures as memories of the school year. Wish each student the best of luck for the upcoming year, and encourage him to keep in touch. The student will be delighted to receive the note and photos, and may send a letter to you in return!

Bonnie Boyd—Gr. 1, Coquina Elementary, Titusville, FL

Thank you, Lara for being a real spark plug in my class! Love, Mrs. Robinson

Special Delivery

A letter from the teacher is always a special treat for students, but this idea will guarantee a special delivery! When writing thank-you notes or letters of encouragement, or returning correspondence, compose your letter on a decorated piece of tagboard. After you have written your letter, carefully cut it into puzzle-piece-shaped sections. Place the pieces into an envelope and send it on its way. Students will be excited to find not only a letter, but a puzzle created especially for them.

Brooke A. Bock—Gr. 2, Lincoln Elementary, Tyrone, PA

Neon Notes

Signal a special assignment with a colorful reminder—a neon notebook! Use a piece of bright-colored construction paper to create a folder bearing the title "Neon Notes." The notebook can be sent home with a different student each day. Clip special instructions to the inside of the folder so that parents are aware of the assignment. One week you may ask for a newspaper article to share with the class; the next week you might request a picture with parallel lines. Provide time for students to discuss their assignments with the class. By the time everyone has had a chance to take the folder home, the class has shared a wealth of knowledge!

Joyce Anarumo—Gr. 3, Public School 45, Staten Island, NY

Go For The Green!

To ensure that homework and important papers end up where they are supposed to, supply each student with a sturdy green take-home folder. The color green will help students learn that green means *go;* the folder *goes* with them to each class, *goes* home with them at the end of the day, then *goes* back to school in the morning. Parents will know to check the folder each night to look for assignment and notes. Correspondence to the teacher can also be sent via the folder, providing a reliable link between home and school. With this simple method, all systems are go for a great school year!

Helen D. Gromadzki—Grs. 1–3, Bollman Bridge Elementary School, Jessup, MD

Box It Up!

Entice students to keep track of their homework papers with a specially designed box that can't be overlooked. Ask each student to bring a large shoebox to school. Provide construction paper, glue, markers, glitter, and stickers for students to use in decorating their boxes. Inform parents that papers sent home in the box are assigned as homework. After the student completes the assignment, the papers should be placed back in the box to be returned to school the next day. Encourage each student to designate a place to keep the box at home so that it will be easy to find even on the most hectic school mornings. With this big, bright reminder, homework assignments will find their way back to school each day.

Author Quilt

Put a favorite author on display with this student-made quilt activity. After sharing several stories written by a selected author, ask children to illustrate their favorite scenes from the stories. Provide a sheet of drawing paper and an assortment of markers for each student. Have several of the storybooks handy for students to refer to as they draw. Arrange the completed illustrations on a large piece of bulletin-board paper to resemble blocks on a quilting pattern. Use a marker to add stitch marks around each square. Display the finished project in your library center or reading area. Your students will be "sew" proud of their literary masterpieces!

adapted from an idea by Melissa Goldenberg
Oak Hill Elementary
Overland Park, KS

Strega Nona
by Tomie dePaola

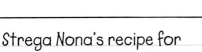

Strega Nona's recipe for pasta is:

Oh, The Books We Have Read!

Start a collection of literary memories with this adaptable activity for any story. After reading a story with your class, distribute a 5" x 7" index card to each student. Instruct the students to write the title and author, and to draw an illustration on one side of the card. On the other side, assign a character sketch, writing assignment, or other activity that relates to the book. Store the completed cards on a metal binder ring, and display them in your library center. Students will enjoy looking back through books you've read together and will be amazed by the volumes of literature they've experienced!

Therese Hillman—Gr. 3
Burgess Elementary School
Sturbridge, MA

Character Portraits

Put your students' artistic abilities to work to create a character sketch-within-a-sketch. Begin by asking each student to make a portrait of a storybook character on white construction paper. Then have her fashion a frame by gluing a strip of brown construction paper to each side of the portrait. Instruct the student to write a sentence about the character on three sides of the frame and the character's name on the fourth side as shown. The result will be a drawing of the character framed by its description—and a gallery of good work.

Peggy Seibel—Gr. 2
St. Mary's School
Ellis, KS

Sequencing Screen

Tune in to sequencing practice with this prime-time idea. Begin by having each student construct a TV set from a 9-inch paper plate. Instruct the student to fold the plate in half and cut a 3-inch slit down each side as shown. Unfold the plate and draw in details such as volume controls and the on/off switch. If desired, attach a pipe-cleaner antennae to the top. Provide each student with a sheet of white construction paper and instruct him to cut it in half lengthwise. Tape the ends together to create a long strip of paper. Direct students to draw pictures representing the beginning, the middle, and the end of the story. Thread the strip of paper through the slits in the paper plate, and have students "broadcast" the story in sequential order. Keep the TV sets handy—when it's time to review sequencing skills, students can write the script for another story.

Marsha Weiner—Gr. 2
Churchill School
Homewood, IL

Word Rings

Motivate students to review their vocabulary words by providing easy access to their word cards. Supply each student with a large metal ring. When new vocabulary words are introduced, have each student copy the words onto individual word cards. Help the student punch a hole in each card and store it on his metal ring. The ring can then be hung on the back of the student's chair. Encourage students to review the word cards when they have a few extra minutes between assignments. You'll be surprised at how often the students study the new vocabulary words!

Karla Gribben—Gr. 1
Chartiers Valley Primary School
Bridgeville, PA

Postcard Vocabulary

Let a picture inspire a thousand words—or at least 10 to 20! Collect a supply of postcards with varied pictures on the front, or have students bring postcards from home. Distribute a postcard to each student and direct him to create a list of 10 to 20 words relating to the picture on the card. Display the cards and word lists for students to observe; then instruct each student to choose a card and use the word list to write a story about the picture. Provide time for each student to share his story, asking the class to identify the postcard that inspired the story. Who would have thought that vocabulary enrichment and context clues could fit on a postcard?

Tracey Quezada
Presentation of Mary Academy
Hudson, NH

Word List

1. Statue Of Liberty
2. skyscrapers
3. harbor
4. boats
5. ocean
6. sky
7. clouds
8. New York
9. Staten Island
10. city
11. book
12. crown
13. gold
14. robe
15. windows
16. flame
17. statue
18. copper
19. buildings
20. tours

Couch-Potato Awards

Motivate students to share their responses to literature with the promise of turning them into couch potatoes! When a student has completed an independent reading, encourage him to write down a few sentences about his reaction to the book. Invite him to share this response with the class followed by a brief question-and-answer session about the book. Award the student with a "Couch Potato" certificate, which allows him to sit on a couch or special area during silent reading time. Your class will be introduced to a variety of literature, and will enjoy the opportunity to be the class couch potato!

Kristen McLaughlin—Gr. 1
Daniel Boone Area School District
Boyertown, PA
and Lee McLaughlin
Boyertown Area School District
Boyertown, PA

COUCH-POTATO AWARD

To: Daniel

Ms. McLaughlin

Guest Reader Recognition

Honor guest readers in your classroom by recording their visits on a permanent bulletin-board display. When a guest reader visits your classroom, take a picture of her holding the book she has shared. Then have her autograph a large book cutout that is mounted on your bulletin board. Arrange each reader's picture on the display. Students will be inspired to look for the books featured in the photos on their trips to the library and will want their friends and family members to be added to the display of literary guests. Your guests may even request a return visit!

Janet Zeek—Gr. 2
Tolleson Elementary School
Tolleson, AZ

Rain Forest Readers

Entice readers to your book corner by turning it into a rain forest adventure! Assemble a small tent in a quiet corner of the classroom and furnish it with a clip-on reading light, several pillows, and a collection of books relating to the rain forest theme. Display a rain forest poster or an arrangement of cutouts on the wall behind the tent, then add a tangle of artificial vines. Invite students to visit the center and travel to the rain forest on the wings of a good book.

Becky Thurlkill—Gr. 3
Junction City Elementary
Junction City, AR

Reader Of The Week

Make sure each student has an opportunity to show off reading skills during the year with a "Reader Of The Week" program. After you have had a chance to assess each student's reading ability, schedule the list of readers. Students who are comfortable reading aloud can be at the top of the list, while students needing more practice can be scheduled for a time later in the year. Send a list of names and dates home with each student, along with a set of guidelines for parents. Encourage the child to choose a book that is suitable in length, has appropriate vocabulary, and will be of interest to the class. A week before the student is scheduled to read, send a reminder note home. When the day arrives, write an announcement on the board with the reader's name and book title. Make sure all readers get a round of applause, and if possible, snap a picture of the child reading to the class. Send it home as a special keepsake of a proud day.

Cindy Marsh—Gr. 2
Midway Elementary
Holt, MI

Joseph is our guest reader today. He will be reading Frog And Toad Are Friends.

Phonics Hunt

Reinforce phonics instruction with a search for sounds. After introducing a new phonics concept to the class, provide a supply of magazines and newspapers for students to peruse in search of the featured sound. Instruct students to cut out words containing the letter or phonics pattern, then glue the examples to a large piece of bulletin-board paper. Display the completed word bank in the classroom and encourage students to add to the list as they find additional examples at home or at school. Students will be on the lookout for phonics all day long!

Leigh Anne Newsom, E. W. Chittum Elementary, Chesapeake, VA

ph	st	f**a**ce long A	br	sh
phone	STREET	case	broke	shield
GRAPH	stop	race	BRAIN	SHOOK
	stomp		bruise	shoot

Phonics Highlight

To help students locate phonics concepts on worksheets and papers, provide each student with a highlighting pen. Direct students to find specified initial consonants, blends, and vowel sounds. As reading skills progress, have students highlight the main idea and topic sentence in a passage. Students will enjoy marking the text with the bright colors, and you'll enjoy the ease in checking their work.

Tracie Smithwick-Rodriguez—Gr. 2, Lexington Elementary School, Corpus Christi, TX

Today is Monday, September 7. Today's weather is hot and sunny. Alice's grandmother brought her a new doll for her birthday. Alice loves her doll.
Sam went to see the circus on Saturday.

Show-And-Tell Phonics

Roll a phonics lesson and a show-and-tell session into one great activity. Begin the lesson by asking students to dictate a sentence about something they want to share with the class. Record the responses on chart paper, then use the resulting text for a phonics lesson. Challenge students to find words with a specific vowel sound, a blend, or an initial consonant. Students circle words on the chart paper or copy the words on individual papers. Because the text changes with each lesson, previous phonics skills can be reinforced and new skills introduced. And the content of each chart is guaranteed to hold student interest!

Colleen Smith—Gr. 1, Moss School, Metuchen, NJ

Book Chat

Provide a comfortable setting for your students to share their responses to reading and generate interest in new books at the same time. Immediately following silent reading time, invite students to sit in a circle and discuss their reading selection. In turn, each student holds up his book and briefly describes its plot. Encourage reluctant speakers with questions about characters and settings. After everyone has had a turn to share, ask students if they heard about a book that interests them. Remind students to look for these books on the next visit to the library. Your students will be eager to explore new books that have been recommended by their classmates.

Cindy Marsh—Gr. 2
Midway Elementary
Holt, MI

Magic Microphone

Encourage students to take center stage as they discuss characters, setting, and story plots. Set the stage for discussion by constructing a microphone from a paper-towel tube and a Styrofoam® ball. Glue the ball to the tube, then spray it with silver spray paint. When it's dry, attach a piece of yarn to the tube to resemble the microphone cord. Ask a student volunteer to step into the spotlight to describe the main character in a story, or to tell about a problem the character faced. Have him pass the microphone to a student wishing to add to the discussion. Be prepared for an enthusiastic response as students take their turns to step up to the mike!

Diane Vogel—Gr. 3
W. B. Redding School
Lizella, GA

Take A Look

Encourage language and vocabulary development with an activity centered on a picture frame. Purchase a large picture mat or construct a cardboard frame. Attach a magnet to the back and place the frame on the chalkboard. Each day select a picture to slip behind the frame. (Calendar art, reprints of famous works, and magazine covers are excellent sources.) Begin the morning with a discussion of the picture, prompting students to use descriptive words to identify shapes, colors, and subjects in the picture. List responses on the board so that students can refer to the list during the day. Before long, your students' vocabularies will be works of art!

Patricia Neal—Gr. 1
Wekiva Elementary
Longwood, FL

beautiful
blue water
tiny seashells
tall sand castles

Suddenly Bob realized he forgot to mow the lawn last month.

When I was a young p... it took days to walk to school.

Comic Connection

Reading and vocabulary reinforcement can be a barrel of laughs when you use the comic section of a newspaper for a learning-center activity. Scan the newspaper for single-frame comics. When you have collected about a dozen, mount each comic on tagboard; then laminate it for durability. Cut apart the picture from the caption and program for self-checking. Place the pieces in a center and watch as students chuckle their way through a comic/caption matchup. To extend the activity, have students write new captions for the comics. Reading reinforcement will become your students' favorite funny business!

Therese Hillman—Gr. 3
Burgess Elementary School
Sturbridge, MA

Glued On Spelling!

Use this tactile technique to provide spelling practice for your youngsters. Provide each child with as many index cards as spelling words. Have the student use colored glue to write a spelling word on each card. After the glue dries, have him use his finger to trace over each spelling word. For an added activity, instruct each child to trade index cards and guess his neighbor's words by feeling the glue with his fingertips—no peeking allowed!

Cindy Ward—Grs. 1–4, Learning Disabilities Teacher
Yellow Branch Elementary
Rustburg, VA

Spelling Exercise

Here's an active approach to spelling your students will love. To begin, call out a spelling word. Have students stand up and spell the word together, jumping each time they come to a vowel. Continue in the same manner with the remaining spelling words. Invite students to think of alternate actions they could do for vowels, such as clapping or stomping. This activity guarantees a classroom full of active learners!

Leigh Anne Newsom, E. W. Chittum Elementary, Chesapeake, VA

Sensational Spelling

Attract students to better spelling skills with these fun tactile activities:

- Have students manipulate magnetic letters on a metal filing cabinet to spell each word on the spelling list.
- Print each letter of the alphabet on a clothespin. Have students "write" their spelling words by attaching the clothespins in the correct order to a ruler. (Be sure to provide extra clothespins for spelling words that have more than one of the same letter.)
- Have students use chalk to write their spelling words on the school sidewalk.
- Provide students with various colors of pipe cleaners. Instruct students to spell one spelling word at a time by using pipe cleaners to form the letters.

Cindy Ward—Grs. 1–4

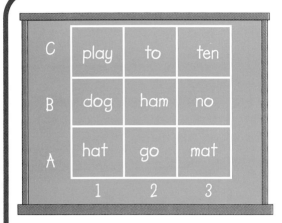

What's The Location?

Improve spelling skills by playing this review game. Draw a large grid on the chalkboard (or overhead projector) with enough squares for each spelling word. Program each square with a spelling word. Then ask students questions regarding the location of the words such as, "What word is at B, 3?" or "What are the coordinates for the word *play?*" Not only are students locating spelling words but they are learning great map skills, too!

Linda Parris—Gr. 1
West Hills Elementary School
Knoxville, TN

Spelling Mailbox

Add a little variety to vocabulary building with a spelling mailbox. Label an old mailbox "Spelling Mailbox" and place a stack of index cards beside it. Instruct students to write down difficult words they come across on index cards and place them in the mailbox. Each Thursday select eight cards from the mailbox and call them out for students to try to write their spellings. Provide a special treat, such as a homework pass or extra computer time, for students spelling four out of the eight words correctly. After reviewing the spellings and definitions of the words, place them on the wall or in an index card file for students to refer to in their writing activities. It won't be long before your students are tackling difficult words with great confidence!

Leigh Anne Newsom, E. W. Chittum Elementary, Chesapeake, VA

Spelling Word Search

Search no further! Here's a spelling activity your youngsters will think is definitely cool! Provide each child with a copy of a blank grid that has enough boxes for each letter of the spelling words. Post a spelling list and ask students to write the spelling words on the grid, one letter in each box. Students will need to add additional letters to fill the extra boxes on the grid. Then have students trade papers with a partner and locate each spelling word. What a great way for students to learn the letters in each spelling word—searching for one letter at a time!

Lorraine LoGuidice—Gr. 1
Franklin Elementary School
Saddle Brook, NJ

Find:
brown   friend
red   send
year   real

b	r	n	o	f	t	w
r	e	d	f	r	w	y
o	a	n	p	i	q	e
w	l	b	u	e	u	a
n	o	d	s	n	i	r
r	s	e	n	d	t	s

ABC Spelling

The News On Spelling

Extra! Extra! Read all about it! Here's an idea for practicing spelling words at a center. Cut several old newspapers into 5" x 7" pieces. Place the newspaper pieces, several highlighter pens, and a numbered copy of the weekly spelling words at the center. Have each child use one of the newspaper cutouts to search letter-by-letter for the spelling words. To begin, the child locates the first letter in the first spelling word and highlights it. He then searches for and highlights the second letter in the word. The student continues in this sequential manner until he has located all the letters in the word. The child then alternates his color of highlighter pen and searches for the letters in the second spelling word. He continues at this center until he locates the letters in all the spelling words. What a novel approach to recycling newspapers—spelling practice!

Tonya Byrd—Grs. 2–3
E. Melvin Honeycutt Elementary
Fayetteville, NC

1. start
2. plan
3. there
4. which
5. please

Midland Reporter-Telegram

Bottled water—"once considered the refreshment of the affluent," as described in FDA Consumer magazine a few years ago—has become a staple for may Americans.

Last year, Americans consumed 2.7 billion gallons of bottled water or about 163 eight-ounce servings persons, according to a bottled water trade association. The record year for consumption and growing popularity are attributed to taste, safety and recognition of bottled water as stand-alone beverage.

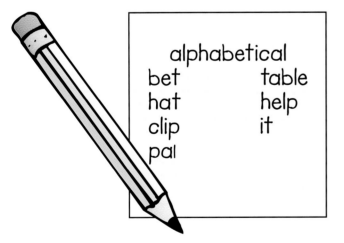

alphabetical
bet   table
hat   help
clip   it
pal

2 letter words = 1 point
3 letter words = 2 points
4 letter words = 3 points
5 or more letter words = 5 points

Spelling Breakdown

This timed game creates a variety of new vocabulary words. Divide the class into several small groups. Supply each group with one pencil and one piece of paper. To begin, write a long word, such as *alphabetical,* on the chalkboard. Each group has five minutes to cooperatively create as many words as they can, using only the letters in the word on the chalkboard. When time is up, have a member from each group read their list of words to the class. Then have each group calculate their points for valid words using the scoring system shown. Award a treat to the group that "breaks down" the most words.

Leigh Anne Newsom
E. W. Chittum Elementary
Chesapeake, VA

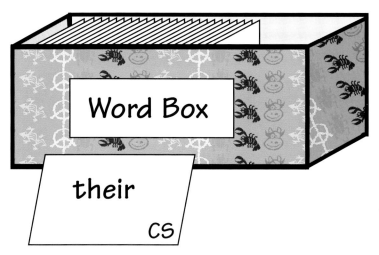

The Word Box

This class word box fosters spelling skills. Before a student requests a word's spelling, he checks for it in the Word Box. If the word is not already filed, write the word and the child's initials on an index card. The child then writes the word in a sentence on the back of the card and returns the card to you to check. After the sentence has been checked, the student alphabetically files his index card in the Word Box. Students refer to the Word Box during daily journal time and other writing opportunities. The best part of all is that as the Word Box grows throughout the school year, so do your youngsters' vocabularies!

Jill Lieberman—Gr. 2
Bedford Village Elementary School
Bedford Village, NY

Recycled Spelling

These nifty cans make learning to spell difficult words easier. At the beginning of the year, request that students bring to school an empty coffee can. Have each child decorate her can and label it "[Student's name]'s Recycled Word Bin." Duplicate several copies of the can pattern on page 158 and place them on a table along with several dictionaries. Whenever a student needs to know how to spell a word, she looks it up in the dictionary, writes the word on a can cutout, and places it in her recycled word bin. Students enjoy using their spelling bins and quickly become very resourceful spellers.

Charlene Afflitto—Grs. 1–2
Grandview Elementary School
Verona, NJ

Telephone Spelling

Ring, Ring! Dial up some spelling practice with this unique activity that combines spelling and math. Duplicate a copy of the telephone keypad on page 158 for each student. (Letters *Q* and *Z* are included with zero.) Display a list of the spelling words and ask each child to copy the first word onto a piece of paper. The student uses the telephone keypad to determine the number assigned to each letter in the spelling word. He then adds the numbers up to determine the word's total number. The student continues in this manner with the remaining spelling words. Be on the lookout for better spelling and addition skills!

Lynn K. Wagner—Gr. 2
J. F. Burns Elementary
Kings Mills, OH

1	2 ABC	3 DEF
4 GHI	5 JKL	6 MNO
7 PRS	8 TUV	9 WXY
	0 QZ	

today
8+6+3+2+9=<u>28</u>

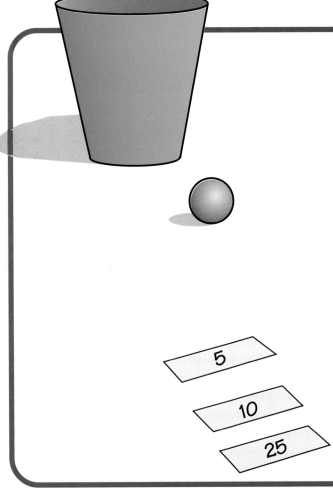

Spelling Toss

This spelling game will score many points with your students. In advance, set up a clean trash can and mark the floor with masking tape as shown. Divide the class into two teams and choose a student from one team to go first. Call out a spelling word to the student. If he spells the word correctly, he gets to try to earn points for his team by tossing a soft ball into a trash can. He may toss the ball from the 5, 10, or 25 point marker. If he makes it, he receives that amount of points. If he misses the trash can, that same amount is subtracted from the team's total. If the student spells the word incorrectly, ask another member on his team to try to spell the word. Continue playing in this manner, alternating between the two teams. The team with the most points at the end of a designated time wins.

Leigh Anne Newsom
E. W. Chittum Elementary
Chesapeake, VA

Letter-By-Letter Spelling

Looking for a different way to practice spelling? Then try this letter-search activity. Provide each child with a 2" x 6" strip of paper for each spelling word (4" x 6" index cards, cut in half horizontally, work well). Instruct students to look through magazines and newspapers in search of each letter in each spelling word. The student cuts out the letters and glues them on the strips of paper to form the spelling words. For an added activity, students can use their spelling cards to put their spelling words in alphabetical order. Your youngsters will be so intent on finding every letter, they won't even realize that they're practicing their spelling!

Lorraine LoGuidice—Gr. 1
Franklin Elementary School
Saddle Brook, NJ

I'm Thinking Of...

Review spelling words with this game of clues. To begin the game, display the weekly list of spelling words. Then say, "I'm thinking of a word that means [definition of a spelling word]." After giving the clue, call on a volunteer to give the correct word and use it in a meaningful sentence. That student then gives the next clue and calls on a classmate. Continue the game in this manner until each spelling word has been used. For an added challenge, try using the game as a cumulative review of several weeks of spelling lists. Whenever you need a unique way to review spelling with minimal preparation time, you're sure to "think of" this activity!

Mary C. Barron—Gr. 3
Morningside Elementary School
Twin Falls, ID

" I'm thinking of a word that means, a common bird that is often used for its meat and eggs."

1. teach
2. speech
3. cheese
4. pitch
5. chicken
6. chain

A Year's Worth Of Writing

In addition to daily journal writing, use this weekly project to create a year-long collection of writing for each student. Once a week, provide writing paper for each student that is decorated with seasonal or other related artwork. On that paper, have each student write a short story about himself and the events that took place during the week. Then have him color the art on the paper. Store students' weekly writings in folders throughout the school year. As the year nears its end, have each child sequence the pages and bind them into a book. The collection will serve as a keepsake of the events and progress that occurred during the year.

Phyllis Bowling—Gr. 2
Smithville Elementary
Smithville, MS

STOP AND PROOFREAD YOUR WRITING

WARNING WRITING UNDER CONSTRUCTION

CAUTION WRITERS AT WORK

Writing Under Construction

Motivate your students by constructing this creative-writing center. Decorate your writing center as a construction zone by posting bright yellow and orange signs with construction phrases such as "Caution: Writers At Work," "STOP And Proofread Your Writing," or "Warning: Writing Under Construction." Add a hard hat to the decor with a sign stating, "Thinking Caps Must Be Worn Beyond This Point." Finally display students' writing works on a bulletin board with the title "The Writing Zone." Your students will soon be hard at work constructing their best compositions.

Joann Bollinger—Gr. 3
Plains Elementary School
Timberville, VA

Name The Classroom Rules

After you teach your class the rules of the school, assign this creative-writing project as a review. Have each student write his first name vertically in the left margin of his paper. Then ask him to write a school rule to correspond with each letter in his name. Students will be thinking creatively to match the rules to the letters in their names, and you will have an assessment of their knowledge of school rules.

Tracie Smithwick-Rodriguez—Gr. 2
Lexington Elementary
Corpus Christi, TX

Keep the room clean.
Eat politely.
Very neat work is best.
I won't run in the hall.
Never hit.

Colorful Writing

Brighten up your lesson with this student-focused idea. When printing text on the board, write each line using a different color of chalk. Use this method to write spelling lists, daily assignments, poems, instructions, etc. It makes the text colorful and interesting to read, and helps students keep their places when copying to their papers.

Barbara Langford—Gr. 2, Greer Elementary School
Charlottesville, VA

Ladybug
I caught a ladybug in my yard. I put her in a jar. I fed her a leaf. She is cute.

Katie

Sticker Stories

Are you having a problem finding a quick and easy writing activity? Then you'll love this instant solution! Gather the unused stickers you've accumulated and place them in a shoebox. Have each child select a sticker, attach it to a sheet of paper, and write a story about the illustration featured on her sticker. Students will be stuck on these fun-to-write sticker stories.

Cereal-Box Promotion

Boost students' creativity with these clever cereal-box covers. Wrap empty cereal boxes with bulletin-board or plain packaging paper. Have each student invent a new type of cereal, then use crayons or markers to design an eye-catching box that promotes his tasty creation. Be sure students write about nutritional information as well as taste appeal. These creations will look good enough to eat.

Daily Math Journal

Engage your students in this twist on journal writing, and reinforce the importance of math. Begin with a discussion about typical things that require math, such as noting the time for a television show, or making supper using a recipe. Once a day, have each child write about ways she used math at school and at home. As students become familiar with math's influence in their daily lives, you will see their journals become more elaborate.

Linda Abshier—Gr. 2, Lometa I.S.D., Lometa, TX

Flip And Read

Try this fun approach to retelling a story. Put one line or portion of the text from a familiar story or song on a large blank drawing page. Continue this process, using as many pages as necessary to complete the story. Then assign a student, or group of students, to illustrate the text that appears on each page. When the drawings are complete, sequence the pages and use two metal rings to bind the book along the top edge. For a special way to share the finished book, slide a wooden dowel through both rings and enlist two volunteers to hold the book as shown. Have your helpers flip each page while the whole class reads the story.

Janet Zeek—Gr. 2, Tolleson Elementary School, Tolleson, AZ

Imagine That!

Add some interest to an ordinary writing project with this imaginative idea! Ask your students to put on their thinking caps and decide on an imaginary career cat such as doctor cat, electrician cat, teacher cat, or baker cat. Next have students write a descriptive story telling the adventures of his career cat. Then give each student a cat-shaped, construction-paper cutout, and provide decorating materials such as sequins, fabric scraps, ribbon, construction paper, and feathers. Have each child decorate both sides of his cat to represent his chosen career. The students will love investigating careers in this unusual way and will be delighted to see their stories and cat decorations displayed in the classroom.

Debra Bousman—Gr. 3
Factory Shoals Elementary School
Douglasville, GA

Picture This!

Write a story about this picture.

Did you tell...
• what is happening
• where it happened
• how it happened

Now check your story for...
✔ spelling
✔ capital letters
✔ punctuation
✔ your name

Picture-Perfect Writing!

Put an end to the often-repeated phrase, "I don't know what to write about!" with this easy-to-make writing center. First snap candid photographs of special classroom and school activities. To create the center, color, cut out, and glue a construction-paper camera to the front of a file folder. Inside the folder draw a picture frame slightly larger than a Press-On Pocket, and write student directions and guidelines. Laminate the folder; then place a Press-On Pocket inside the frame. Put a photograph inside the pocket. When desired, replace the existing photograph and you have a brand-new writing center—personalized with your students' smiling faces!

Graphing Table

Here's the perfect way to have a graph permanently available to use in your classroom. Use colored electrical tape to divide a rectangular table into a grid. Then have students gather around the table to put the graph to use. Create an instant lesson by adding labels, providing markers, and having each student add to a square in the graph; then discuss the results.

Tracie Smithwick-Rodriguez—Gr. 2
Lexington Elementary
Corpus Christi, TX

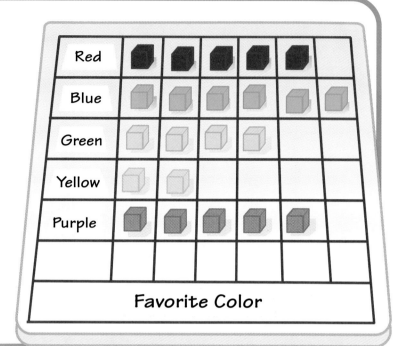

Graphing Made Easy

Here's another great graphing idea! Cover a class supply of juice can lids with construction paper—one color for girls and one color for boys. Personalize a lid for each child; then glue a magnet on the back of each lid. Store the lids on a magnetic chalkboard or file cabinet. Whenever you wish to graph students' preferences or opinions, write the choices on the chalkboard or on labels for the file cabinet. Then have each child display his lid in the appropriate place on the graph. What a quick and easy solution to graphing!

Kelly Carrier—Gr. 1
Clarkmoor Elementary School
Sumner, WA

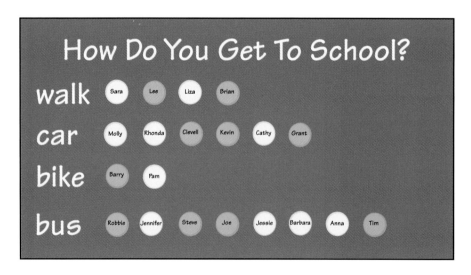

Wheel Of Multiplication

Reinforce multiplication facts by creating multiplication wheels. To make a wheel, write each number 0–9 twice (in random order) around the edge of a small paper plate. Cut an arrow using poster board and attach it to the center of the plate using a brad. On the arrow, write a number to represent the set of facts you want practiced. Instruct each child to take the wheel home and say each fact to a parent as he spins the wheel. Once the facts are learned, a student should be able to complete the wheel in 30 seconds or less. Your students will appreciate this new spin on learning multiplication facts.

Joann M. Bollinger—Gr. 3
Plains Elementary School
Timberville, VA

Race To 100

Try this exciting, fast-paced math race to get your students turned on to addition. Each child needs a pencil, a sheet of paper, and a die. When the race begins, each child tosses his die and writes down the number on his paper. He then tosses the die again and adds that number to the first. On the third toss, the number is added to the previous sum. All the children continue to race in this manner (each tossing and adding at his own pace) until one child reaches or exceeds 100. That child calls out, "Winner," and everyone must stop while you quickly check his addition. This game will bring out a winning spirit in your classroom and strengthen addition skills too!

Leslie Poythress—Gr. 3
Gray Elementary School
Gray, GA

Giant Number Line

Students will love practicing their facts using a huge number line. To make the number line, purchase a vinyl tablecloth with felt backing. Cut it lengthwise into strips measuring about 18" in width. (The width and the length of the strips will vary depending on the size of the tablecloth.) Then sew the ends of the strips together to make one long strip. Next cut the actual line and the numbers out of a solid-color Con-Tact® paper and attach them to the tablecloth strip to form the number line. Now invite your youngsters to walk, hop, skip, or jump out their addition or subtraction problems.

Angie Cullin—Gr. 2, St. Susanna School, Plainfield, IN

Roll 'em!

Add some pizzazz to math facts with these large dice. Cover two cube-shaped boxes with white paper. Program each side of the dice with colored stickers for dots or a permanent marker for numbers; then cover the dice with clear Con-Tact® paper for durability. Have students roll the dice to determine a variety of math fact problems. Not only are the box dice cheap and easy to make—they're quieter too!

Mary Kay Gallagher—Gr. 1
Seton Catholic School
Moline, IL

The Change Game

This kid-pleasing game will teach your students about counting change. To make the gameboard, use colored tape to divide a sheet of poster board into a grid. Cut pictures from a magazine or catalog and glue one item in each section of the grid. Cut out and glue a price tag in each section reflecting a price of less than 25 cents. To play the game, divide the class into groups of four, and place the grid on the floor. Distribute $1.00 and four beanbags to each group. Have the members of one team each toss a beanbag onto the grid. The items where the beanbags land are that team's purchases. The team must add up the total cost of the purchased items and then determine how much change they will receive from their dollar. Give each team an opportunity to toss the beanbags and figure their change. The team that receives the most change wins!

Amy Flanigan—Substitute Teacher
Garrett County School System
Mt. Lake Park, MD

10¢	12¢	18¢	15¢
5¢	20¢	24¢	21¢
22¢	4¢	12¢	9¢
7¢	11¢	14¢	22¢
22¢	6¢	13¢	20¢

Items	Cost
Cheeseburger	79¢
Small Fries	85¢
Chocolate Shake	99¢
Subtotal	$2.63
Tax (5%)	.13
Total Cost	$2.76

Fast-Food Facts

Your students will be anxious to put their math skills to work to determine a purchase from a favorite fast-food restaurant. Obtain a menu or price list from a nearby fast-food restaurant. Duplicate a class supply. Give each student a copy of the menu and ask him to select the items he would like for a lunch. Have him record his purchases and find the sum of the selected items. Then help each child add the sales tax to determine the total cost of his meal. When the orders have been chosen, plan a field trip to the restaurant for lunch. Have each child bring his order and the required amount of money. What a treat for completing a unit about money!

Carol Merchant—Gr. 2
Barnaby Manor Elementary
Oxon Hill, MD

Book-Order Math

Do you receive duplicates of monthly book-order forms from children's book clubs? If so, don't toss them out. Recycle them to teach a hands-on money lesson. Distribute an order form to each child. Invite the child to choose books that he would like to purchase. (If desired, place a maximum on the number of books that can be ordered.) Then have him fill out an order form and mark the books he chose. Next have the student calculate the total cost of his order. (If needed, have students use calculators.) When each student has determined his total, instruct him to collect that amount of money from a class bank filled with plastic coins and paper dollars. Have each child place his money and book-order form in an envelope and give it to you to check. Not only will students gain practice counting money; they'll learn the process of ordering books, too!

Beth Dordick—Gr. 2, Woodland Primary West, Gages Lake, IL

BOOK CLUB

Item #	Titles	Paid Items	Price	Amount Paid
TEC111	Facts About Animals		$1.50	
TEC121	Facts About Sports		$1.50	
TEC131	Facts About The Human Body		$1.50	
TEC141	Shaggy Dog Shades	1	$1.25	$1.25
TEC154	Paddlin' Penguins	1	$1.35	$1.35
TEC165	Teddy Bear's Bakery	1	$1.35	$1.35
TEC171	The Bumblebee Bunch		$1.50	
TEC175	Bag Of Bones		$1.00	
TEC178	Toy Box Rock	2	$1.00	$2.00
TEC180	Kangaroo Clock	1	$1.50	$1.50
TEC185	The Gingerbread House		$1.50	
TEC190	Mr. Fancy Pants		$1.20	
TEC200	Prairie Puppies		$1.40	
TEC205	Rockin' Horse Riders		$1.60	
TEC210	Camp Pup Tent	1	$1.00	$1.00
TEC215	Teddy Bears And Bow Ties		$1.90	
TEC221	Three Peas In A Pod		$1.35	
TEC230	Blossom The Opossum		$1.55	
		7		$8.45
		Total Paid Items		Total Amount Paid

Operation Needed!

Resuscitate math lessons with a visit from the doctor. A few times each month introduce math lessons by dressing up as a doctor. Put on a white lab coat and a toy stethoscope. You will also need a toy doctor's bag in which to place math problems needing operations. To make the math problems, write five addition or subtraction word problems on index cards; then place the cards in the doctor's bag. (Be sure to include your students' names in the word problems.)

To begin the lesson, disguise your voice and introduce yourself to your students as "Doctor [your last name]." Ask them if they would like to help with today's operations. Draw a card from your doctor's bag and read the word problem. Then ask the students, "What operation does this patient need—addition or subtraction?" Call on a volunteer to answer the question. Reward a correct response with a small Band-Aid® or a piece of LifeSavers® candy. Continue in this manner with the other four cards; then say good-bye to the students. When you return as their teacher, your students are sure to be prepped up and ready for a math lesson.

Mary B. Decker—Gr. 2, St. Michael School, Netcong, NJ

B. Decker, M.D.

Jared has 18 video games. Sean has 12 video games. How many more video games does Jared have than Sean?

Numerous Numbers

Make math more enticing to your students by reading aloud *Math Counts: Numbers* by Henry Pluckrose. This book relates numbers to the real world by showing them in varied situations from car license plates to numbers on an athlete's shirt. After sharing the book with your students, distribute a piece of colored construction paper and a magazine to each child. Have him look for pictures that include numbers in some way, cut them out, and then glue them to his paper. After each child shares his page of numbers, compile the pages into a class book titled "Numerous Numbers." Students will see that math definitely counts in their lives!

Kathleen Geddes Darby—Gr. 1
Community School
Cumberland, RI

Friendship Mix

Here's a tasty technique for teaching measurements that is sure to hold your students' attention. Ask each child to bring to school a small amount of a bite-size snack item such as cereal, pretzels, nuts, or chocolate chips. (Do not tell them what the snacks will be used for.) On the day of the lesson, have students estimate the weight and volume of their snacks in ounces, grams, and cups. Instruct each child to weigh and measure his snack and then record the amounts on a large chart. After students finish measuring, explain to students that all things taste better when they are shared; then combine all the snacks in a very large bowl or bag and mix. Invite each child to measure a cup of the friendship mix to eat and enjoy. Yum, yum! Now that's a tasteful math lesson!

Pam Wilson—Gr. 3, Ebenezer School, Statesville, NC

Estimation Station

Make this estimation activity a part of your students' daily routine. Create a bulletin board with the heading "Estimation Station." Attach five plastic jars to the board using Velcro®, and label each jar with a day of the school week. Partially fill each jar with small objects such as jelly beans. For your daily estimation lesson, take the appropriate jar off the bulletin board and pass it to each student in the room. Allow each child to estimate how many objects he believes are in the jar. Record student responses using an overhead projector so all students are able to view the results. Include the previous day's number in your discussion to give children a reference on which to base the day's estimation. For example you might say, "There were 26 jelly beans in the container yesterday. Today there are more jelly beans in the jar." To conclude, ask students to sort the objects into portion cups by fives or tens, then have them count the total number.

Linda Parris—Gr. 1
West Hills Elementary School
Knoxville, TN

Seasonal Counters

Add color to your students' counting with this great tip. Purchase a medium-size clay flowerpot and several bags of dry lima beans for each holiday or season. Paint the inside and outside of each flowerpot and bag of beans with a holiday-related color. After the beans dry, place them in their corresponding flowerpot. Try orange and black counters in an orange flowerpot for Halloween. Or try a gold pot and gold counters for a St. Patrick's Day pot of gold nuggets. The students will have a variety of colorful counters to use when practicing addition, subtraction, and place value.

Sarah Mertz—Grs. 1–2, Owenton, KY

Fruity Fraction Feast

Make math simply delicious with this idea for introducing fractions! On the day before teaching the lesson, ask each child to bring a fruit to school the next day. Begin the lesson by sharing *Eating Fractions* by Bruce McMillan with your youngsters. After reading the story, provide each child with a plastic knife, a paper plate, toothpicks, and small strips of paper. Have students cut their fruits into equal pieces. Instruct each child to write a fraction for each piece of fruit on the paper strips and tape them to the toothpicks. Then have the student place a labeled toothpick in each piece of fruit. Invite students to share their fractions with the class before feasting on these fabulous fraction snacks.

Susan Rodgers—Gr. 3, Tuckerton Elementary School, Tuckerton, NJ

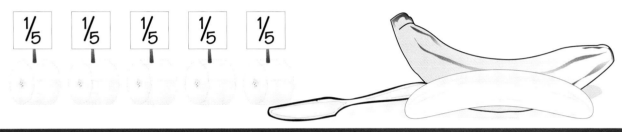

Math Tic-Tac-Toe

Looking for a way to add excitement to your math reviews? Then try this whole-group activity. Provide each child with a lap chalkboard and a piece of chalk. (Paper and pencils work fine also.) Then draw a tic-tac-toe grid on the chalkboard and write a math problem in each box. Divide the class into two teams. Assign one group to be the *X*s and one group to be the *O*s. Call on one student from team X to choose a box. Instruct each student in the class to solve the problem on her chalkboard. Before students show their answers, choose one student from each team to stand by you at the chalkboard. Then ask the other students to show their answers. If the student standing by you from team X has the correct answer, have her put an *X* in that box on the board. If her answer is incorrect, the student standing beside you from team O has the opportunity to put an *O* in the box if his answer is correct. Continue in this manner, alternating between both teams, until one team has tic-tac-toe—three correct answers in a row!

Nancy Lujan—Gr. 3, C. I. Waggoner Elementary School, Tempe, AZ

**Math**

Place Value On The Overhead

Give place value a new look with these inexpensive, overhead manipulatives. Purchase a plastic, needlepoint grid square at your local craft store. Cut the square into grids of 100 squares, columns of 10 squares, and single ones. Place the manipulatives on the overhead projector and project on the screen. What an easy solution to the problem of expensive overhead manipulatives!

Deanna M. Noser—Gr. 2
Warfield Elementary School
Indiantown, FL

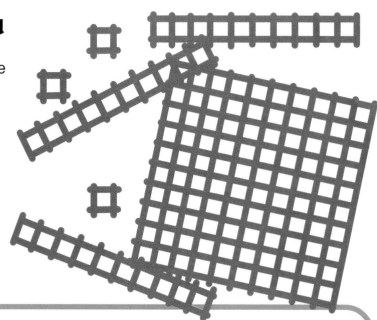

Place-Value Utensils

Utensils aren't just for eating with—they can help teach the value of digits, too! Purchase a silverware tray and a box of plastic knives, forks, and spoons. Use a permanent marker to write "100" on each knife, "10" on each fork, and "1" on each spoon. Then write those same numbers on the appropriate slots in the tray. Set the tray and a predetermined number of each utensil, less than ten, at a table. Next have a small group of students sort the utensils, placing each utensil in its appropriate slot. After sorting, have students count and record the number of each type of utensil. Then have students determine a total number using the information recorded. For example 5 knives, 8 forks, and 3 spoons would be 583. Continue the activity with the other small groups until each student has had a chance to help sort the utensils. Students will be more than ready to dig into this activity!

Kathy Martin
Nellie Reed School
Vernon, MI

knives 5 forks 8 spoons 3 = 583

Ziti Place Value

Combine jewelry making and place value for a one-of-a-kind math lesson. Supply each child with 21 to 29 ziti noodles and two lengths of yarn. If desired, dye the noodles with a mixture of rubbing alcohol and food coloring. Instruct each child to sort his noodles into groups of tens and ones. Have him string each group of ten noodles on a length of yarn; then tie a knot to form a bracelet. (Each child should have two bracelets and one to nine leftover noodles.) Ask each child to share how many tens and ones he has, tell his total number of noodles, and then show his bracelets to the class. Students will leave this lesson with two bracelets and a greater understanding of place value.

Amy Smith—Gr. 2
King And Queen Elementary
Williamsburg, VA

2 tens and
4 ones = 24

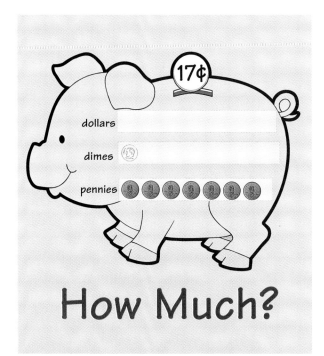

17¢

dollars

dimes

pennies

How Much?

A Penny A Day

Students will go-hog wild over this activity that keeps track of the school days and practices money skills at the same time. Enlarge, color, and cut out the pig pattern and attached coin on page 159; then laminate for durability. Attach three pieces of Velcro® to the pig and label as shown. Next attach Velcro® to the tails side of ten pennies, nine dimes, and one silver dollar. On the first day of school, use a wipe-off marker to write "1¢" on the coin; then add one penny to the row labeled "pennies." Each day continue to add another penny to the display, until reaching ten pennies. On the following day, trade the ten pennies in for a dime to display on the pig cutout. On the hundredth day of school, cash in the nine dimes and ten pennies for one silver dollar. By the end of the school year, your class will have quite a display of coins and money skills!

Susan May, Harlan School, Florence, AL

Carnation Creation

Impress your students with this colorful science experiment. Begin by purchasing white carnations from your local florist. Then have each student choose a color to dye his flower. In a cup, prepare a mixture of food coloring (in the preferred color) and water for each student. Place each flower in a cup with the mixture, and let it stand for two days. Ask each child to observe her flower several times during the two-day period. She will notice the gradual change as the color is transferred to the flower. For a finishing touch, shorten the flower's stem, then add some fine netting and a bow to create a corsage. Encourage each child to treat her mother, grandmother, or special friend to the beautiful carnation creation.

Deborah Ross—Primary
Wayland Alexander School
Hartford, KY

Schoolwide Science Storage

Many science supplies can be costly or time-consuming to gather. Create a schoolwide resource area for science supplies. Place the supplies in large, clear, plastic storage boxes and label the contents. Stack them in a resource area with a checkout list. When you need to prepare a science lesson in a hurry, chances are the supplies you need can be found in the resource room.

We Hear

Clink, Clink, Bang, Rattle!

Watch your students' curiosities perk up when they hear about this listening experiment. Cover five potato-chip canisters with colorful paper and label each container with a number from one to five. Fill each canister with a different collection of noisy items such as rice, nuts and bolts, paper clips, or marbles. Then place the cans at a learning center and provide paper for students to write their guesses on. Add a prize as an incentive for the most correct guesses. Change the contents of the canisters frequently to renew the experiment.

Mary Kay Gallagher—Gr. 1
Seton Catholic School
Moline, IL

Solid Or Liquid?

Test your students' knowlege of solids and liquids by introducing this mystery mixture. Create a mixture of three parts cornstarch to two parts water. Have each student place a small amount of the gooey mixture in his hand. As the child rolls the mixture, it takes on a doughy, stiff texture. When the student lets the mixture sit in his hand, it suddenly relaxes back to a liquid consistency. Challenge your students to debate whether the mixture is a liquid or a solid by discussing the properties observed.

Sherry Geier—Gr. 1
Silver Elementary School
Olney, IL

Rock Roundup

Don't worry over where to keep all the rocks and stones that students collect during your rock unit. Have each student make a personal rock collection using an egg carton. Encourage each child to decorate or paint the top, then personalize the collection with his name. Challenge students to research each rock that's collected and label each rock's type near its compartment.

Jacob

Science Storage

Help your young scientists stay organized by creating handy science portfolios. At the beginning of each new science unit, distribute a pocket folder to each student. Announce the upcoming science theme and have the children decorate the folders to reflect the unit's topic. During the unit, ask students to store all writing samples, art projects, experiment results, literature lists, etc., in their folders. When the unit comes to a close, you will have a completed portfolio to use as an assessment. Your students will have a well-organized collection of related materials to take home.

Cheryl Goldstein—Grs. 3–5 Developmental Handicap
Columbus Intermediate School
Bedford Heights, OH

Body Works

Help your students depict the inner workings of the human body with life-sized chalk drawings. Pair students; then have each child use white chalk to trace his partner's body on a flat sidewalk surface. Next have each child use colored chalk to add parts such as the heart, lungs, bones, and veins in the appropriate places on his chalk outline. Children will enjoy expressing their knowledge of the human body and you can evaluate their work at a glance.

Catherine Greenslade—Gr. 2
Crosswind Elementary School
Collierville, TN

Perfect Science Catchall

Always keep a supply of 35mm film canisters on hand for a quick science aid. The canisters can quickly become vessels for storing soil samples, insects, or water samples while you're out collecting. The handy snap-on lids insure safekeeping until you return to the classroom. The canisters can also be made into a collection of measuring weights by adding sand or salt. Simply measure the ingredients on a scale for accuracy, label the container, permanently seal the canister, and you instantly have a set of weights to use with a balancing scale.

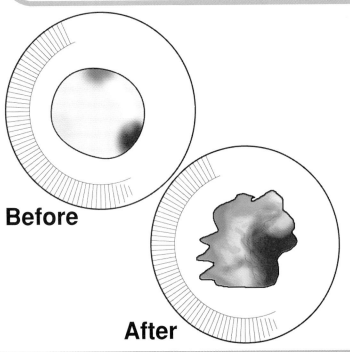

Before

After

Syrup Rainbow

Create all the colors of the rainbow using these simple ingredients. Place two tablespoons of Karo® light corn syrup in the center of a sturdy, white paper plate. Along the syrup's edge, add one drop each of red, blue, and yellow food coloring, forming the points of a triangle with the three drops. Ask a child to slowly stir the syrup to blend the colors, and have your students list new colors as they form. Use this impressive experiment as an introduction to the study of primary and secondary colors.

Lindy Hopkins
Saltillo Elementary School
Saltillo, MS

Take Flight!

Introduce a simple study of aeronautics through the use of paper airplanes. Have each child construct a simple paper airplane. Be sure each student uses the same material. Test-fly the planes and have students note the differences and similarities of each plane's flying pattern. Then supply students with a variety of paper (in different weights and sizes), paper clips, staples, and tape. Challenge students to make planes in a range of sizes, and equip them with a variety of added features. For example, make extra folds or cuts in the plane, or attach paper clips for extra weight. Now have another flight test and note the planes' abilities under the new conditions. Your study of flight will really take off after you land this experiment!

Sherry Geier—Gr. 1
Silver School
Olney, IL

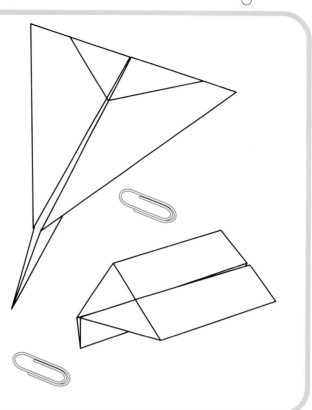

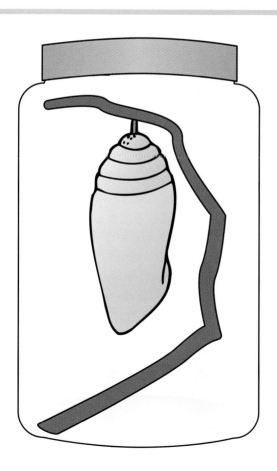

Nature's Wonders

Expose your students to the tiny scientific wonders of nature. During the fall months, take your students on an outdoor excursion in search of cocoons and chrysalises. Collect a few of each, and put them in large jars with ventilation. Place the cocoons and chrysalises where they will receive the same temperature changes as they would in nature. Then have your students make and record predictions about the changes that will take place in the tiny shelters. Ask them to guess what they believe will emerge. As spring approaches, watch for changes daily. When the creatures are revealed, have students reread their predictions and compare them to the results. Challenge students to write a short story to tell about the experience.

Sherry Geier—Gr. 1

State Search

Send your students on a trek across America with a weekly state search. Set the stage for the search with a geography center supplied with a globe, copies of the reproducible on page 160, and reference material for the state featured that week. At the beginning of each week, display a sign at the center to announce the name of a state. Students have the week to visit the center, locate the state on a U.S. map, and complete the activities on the reproducible. At the end of the week, ask student volunteers to share information about the state. In no time at all, your students will have traveled from coast to coast!

Laurie Gibbons—Gr. 1
Elm Street Elementary
Peachtree City, GA

In Honor Of Our Veterans

This distinctive display makes Veterans Day more meaningful to your students by adding a personal touch. A week before Veterans Day, send home a questionnaire asking parents to list the names of the student's relatives who have served in any of the United States armed forces, the years that were served, and the wars that were fought. After you collect the information, have students make a ribbon of honor for each veteran. Arrange the ribbons around the American flag, and invite parents to come see the display. Students will be proud to see the names of their relatives recognized on this important holiday.

Doreen Bednarski—Substitute Teacher
Baldwinsville Central School District
Baldwinsville, NY

Partners In Geography

Pair up with another class for this message-in-a-bottle method of studying geography. At the beginning of the week, have your class write four clues about a geographical location. Include information regarding which side of the equator the location is on, which ocean borders it, or any significant landforms it has. Roll up the clues and place them in a bottle, then deliver to the other class. When the other class has identified the location, they send the bottle back to you. Return the bottle with a message to confirm the answer. The following week, the other class sends four clues your way, and it is your class' turn to search the map. Bon voyage!

Kirsta Davey—Grs. K–3
Nashoba Brooks School
Concord, MA

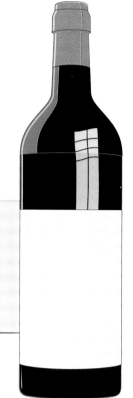

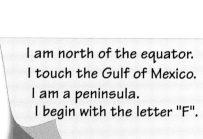

I am north of the equator.
I touch the Gulf of Mexico.
I am a peninsula.
I begin with the letter "F".

Rules Of
Evergreen Island

EVERGREEN ISLAND

Island Adventure

Take your class to a desert isle for an exercise in cooperative teamwork. Divide the class into small groups, and explain that each group is to imagine that they have been dropped off on a deserted island. Assuming the basic needs of food, water, and shelter are taken care of, the group has to decide a name for the island, what rules or laws will be necessary to maintain order on the island, and how the workload will be divided among the inhabitants. Have each group make a banner announcing the name of their island, draw a picture of the island's topography, and create a poster showing the island's rules and division of labor. Provide time for each group to present their project to the class; then display the completed assignments in the hallway. Your class will have so much fun, they may not want to be rescued from their islands!

Kathleen Guide—Gr. 3
St. Ann's School
Raritan, NJ

Earth Day Parade

Earth Day is celebrated in April each year—what a great time for a parade to celebrate the earth in its springtime glory! A week before the event, send a note home with students asking for materials to recycle into banners, signs, and posters for the parade. Items such as shower curtains, sheets, cardboard boxes, and wrapping paper can easily be transformed into message boards bearing slogans for protecting the environment. Have students work on these projects in the week prior to Earth Day. When the special day arrives, have the class parade their creations around the school grounds before displaying their signs in the cafeteria, library, and hallways.

Nancy Lujan—Gr. 3
C. I. Waggoner Elementary School
Tempe, AZ

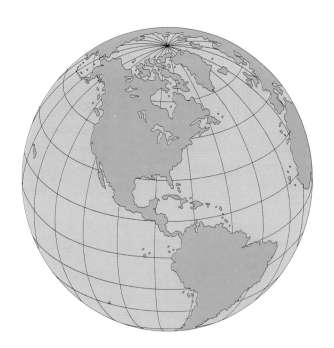

Geographical Lineup

This simple technique for having your class line up will help to reinforce map skills. At the beginning of each week, divide your class into small groups of three or four students; then assign a geographical location to each group. Start out by assigning each group basic map concepts such as one of the cardinal directions. Then throughout the year, progress to more specific locations such as continents, oceans, countries, and states. When it's time for students to get in line, point to an area on the map and announce, "Will China's group please line up?" or, "Everyone in the Atlantic Ocean group may get in line." Students walk by the map and point to their location as they line up. By the end of the year, your students will feel like world travelers!

Michelle Tuinstra—Gr. 2
Lafayette Christian School
Lafayette, IN

Island "Geo-graph-y"

These individual student projects evolve into a graphing activity for the whole class. Begin by providing each student with a portion of air-drying clay and a paper plate. Instruct the students to fashion an island from the clay, then place it on the paper plate to dry. (This may take several days.) Then have each student paint his island and create a list of statistics telling the island's name, topological features, plants and wildlife, and climate. To display the islands, use a large piece of blue bulletin-board paper to represent an ocean. Use masking tape to create a grid on the paper as shown, making sure there is a square on the grid for each student in the class. After each student has had an opportunity to share his project with the class, instruct him to place his island on a specific coordinate of the grid. When all islands have been placed, use the grid to ask questions pertaining to each island's location. Students will enjoy island-hopping to find the answers!

Kirsta Davey—Grs. K–1, Nashoba Brooks School, Concord, MA

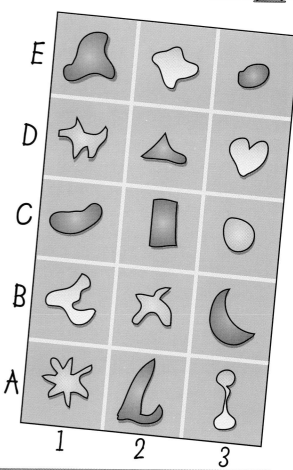

Town Talk

Set the stage for a unit on communities by having students construct a classroom town. Ask students to determine what types of businesses and services a town should offer. List the responses on the board. Then designate a table in your room to be the future site of the new town. Assign each student to be responsible for a business or service in the town, and have him stake its location on the tabletop. Provide a supply of boxes, construction paper, glue, and scissors, and instruct each child to design a building for his establishment. When construction is complete, have students arrange their buildings on the tabletop. Celebrate with a Founder's Day party, where each student describes his contribution to the town, and the class toasts the new community with ginger ale!

Peggy Morin—Gr. 2
Miller School
Wilton, CT

I Spy...Map Skills!

Students love to play the game of I Spy, where they give clues about objects they see in the classroom. Why not use the same game plan to reinforce cardinal directions? Display a large United States map or distribute individual desk maps and announce to the class, "I spy a state south of Oklahoma." Allow time for the students to study their maps; then ask a volunteer to name the state. If the student correctly identifies the state, he leads the next round with clues for another location. I spy...students with great map skills!

Elaine Parr—Gr. 2
Copeland Elementary
Houston, TX

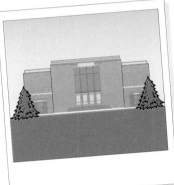

I went shopping for new shoes at this store. I wanted green shoes, but Mom said, "No!"

We eat here when Mom is too tired to cook. I always get a hamburger.

Dad takes me to this park sometimes. One time we flew a kite.

Community Photo Album

Put your students' writing skills to use in this project that highlights places in your community. To begin the study, take some photos of several places of interest in your area. Include snapshots of places your students will be familiar with, such as restaurants, parks, stores, and libraries. Place the pictures and a supply of writing paper in a center. Encourage each student to visit the center and examine the photos, then choose one picture for a writing assignment. The student tells the name of the place in the picture, explains what kind of things happen at that place, describes the sights, sounds, or smells of the place, and mentions any personal experience he has had there. When each student has completed the assignment, bind the pages together into a book about your community. Read the resulting book to your class. Your little authors will know their community inside and out!

Julie Prescott—Gr. 1
Fort Street Elementary
Mars Hill, ME

Continental Camp Out

Take your students to every continent with this classroom camping trip. Purchase a small tent and set it up in a corner of the classroom. Place a sign on the tent announcing the name of a continent. Gather books, posters, postcards, maps, and other resources about the continent, and arrange them inside the tent. Have each student visit the display with a partner to explore the information about the continent. Instruct them to share something they learned about the continent by drawing a picture, writing a paragraph, or creating a list of facts. Keep the students' work on display until it is time to move to another continent; it can then be bound into a booklet of student travels. Your students will cover a lot of territory throughout the school year!

JoAnne Wallis—Gr. 2
Gearing Elementary
St. Clair, MI

"Welcome to Australia"

Oct. ;-)
Today Robert lost a tooth and we learned about bats.

Timeline Links

Introduce students to the concept of a timeline with an idea that links the past to the present. Each afternoon, review the happenings of the day. Use a marker to record the most important event on a strip of construction paper. After forming the first loop of the chain, attach each loop to the previous day's loop. Periodically review several events in the chain and discuss their order of occurrence. At the end of the school year, take the loops apart and discuss the event recorded on each strip. Your students will enjoy remembering past projects, field trips, and special visitors, and you can create a teachable moment by reinforcing the chronological order.

Cornered!

Looking for an indoor game to play next time it rains? Then try this quiet game that involves the entire class. To begin, label each corner of your classroom with a different number or word. Choose a student to be the caller; then have this student close his eyes and count to ten out loud. During this time, each of the remaining students quietly moves to the corner of his choice. After counting to ten, the caller names a corner and then opens his eyes. All students in the called corner must return to their desks. Repeat the process starting with the counting step until only one player remains standing. That student becomes the new caller. What a great way to end recess—with everyone already back in their seats!

Jeannie Hinyard—Gr. 2
Welder Elementary School
Sinton, TX

A Circle Of Friends

Help students get to know each other better and increase self-awareness with this nifty game. All you need is a small ball or potato and music that can be quickly started and stopped. Gather students in a circle on the floor; then give the ball to one student. While the music is playing, the students pass the ball around the circle in a designated direction. The student who is holding the ball when the music stops shares something about himself with the class. Have students continue passing the ball until each student has had a chance to share. The children learn a lot about themselves and their classmates.

Barbara Langford—Gr. 2
Greer Elementary
Charlottesville, VA

"Class-y" Journal

Turn special classroom events into lasting memories with this unique idea. At the end of each week gather your students in a circle on the floor. Ask students to recall things they learned and activities they participated in during the week. Record their responses on a sheet of chart paper. Use a hole puncher to punch holes in the left side of the sheet of chart paper. Add each week's page to a big book labeled "What's Happening In Room [number]?" and use metal rings to compile the book. Store the book in the classroom reading center for students to read and reminisce.

Jody Walsh—Gr. 1
Brookdale Christian School
Bloomfield, NJ

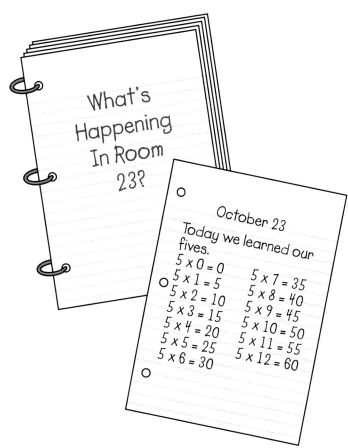

What's Happening In Room 23?

October 23
Today we learned our fives.

$5 \times 0 = 0$
$5 \times 1 = 5$
$5 \times 2 = 10$
$5 \times 3 = 15$
$5 \times 4 = 20$
$5 \times 5 = 25$
$5 \times 6 = 30$

$5 \times 7 = 35$
$5 \times 8 = 40$
$5 \times 9 = 45$
$5 \times 10 = 50$
$5 \times 11 = 55$
$5 \times 12 = 60$

Praises	Concerns	Suggestions
Cathryn helped Mia with her spelling words.	We don't have enough pencils.	Let's play dodgeball next week.

Cooperative Classroom

Add more democracy to your classroom with this cooperative tip. Place a large dry-erase board and pen in an easily accessible area in your classroom. Divide the board into three columns labeled "praises," "concerns," and "suggestions." Invite students to respond to any of the three categories throughout the week. At the end of the week, gather your youngsters for a class meeting. Discuss the suggestions and ask students to help you solve the concerns. At the end of the meeting have an awards ceremony for the students who have been praised by someone in the class. Students will enjoy the chance to make a difference in their classroom!

Carolyn A. Walker—Gr. 2
Bettie F. Williams
Virginia Beach, VA

Dress The Principal

Looking for a one-of-a-kind gift for your school's principal? If so, try this tip! Read aloud *The Principal's New Clothes* by Stephanie Calmenson. After discussing the book, invite your students to design new clothes for the principal. In advance, ask permission from your principal to photocopy his school picture. Place the photograph near the top of a blank sheet of paper and duplicate a copy for each student. Before the designing begins, discuss the many types of outfits students might choose to draw, such as gardening clothes, vacation clothes, or even a bathing suit. Then distribute a photocopy of your principal to each student and let the designing begin. Ask each child to label the parts of clothing he draws. Compile the sheets into a book and have your students present it to the principal for his birthday or as an end-of-the-year present. Students will smile nonstop through this activity and learn that their principal has other interests as well!

Jane M. Smith—Gr. 1
GMG School
Green Mountain, IA

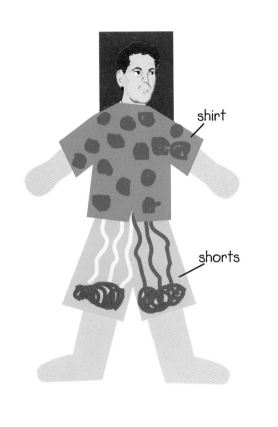

Everyone Has Questions!

Pique your students' interest at the beginning of a new unit of study with this question poster. Label a piece of poster board "Here's my question about [name of unit of study]." Display the poster; then have each student write a question about the unit on the poster. Throughout the course of the unit, incorporate your students' questions into your lesson plans. Have each child place a check beside his question after it has been discussed. Students will feel like they are determining their studies and that will mean a room full of eager listeners for you!

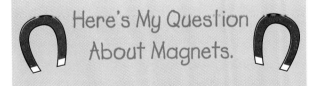

How strong is the strongest magnet?

How do you make a magnet?

Why do magnets only stick to metal?

Lining Up—With Patterns!

How do you get students to line up quickly and quietly? Try some creative ways that not only insure order, but are also unique learning experiences. Ask for silence as you choose students to line up one-by-one to make a pattern. You could choose to line up your students according to their hair color, color of shirt, or type of shoes. Once everyone is in the pattern line, ask for volunteers to guess the pattern. Whoever determines the pattern gets to choose a pattern during the next lineup.

Susan Baker—Gr. 2
Sawgrass Elementary
Sunrise, FL

Money Lineup

Got a few minutes before your class needs to be somewhere? Try lining students up using a little math practice. Choose a denomination of money for your students to be, such as pennies, nickels, or dimes. Once students have lined up, ask them to count their total value. For example, if your students line up as nickels, they would start at the beginning of the line and count by fives until they reach the end of the line. Not only is this activity a five-minute filler, but it's also a good review for money and skip counting!

Claudia Baumann—Gr. 1, Cabrillo Elementary, Hawthorne, CA

Weekly Warm-Up

Start the week off with this great Monday morning icebreaker. Have each student draw a picture of something he did during the weekend. Then ask him to tell a partner about his weekend. After a few minutes, invite each student to share his partner's picture with their classmates. Students will be excited to have an opportunity to share their weekend experiences in this unique way. And they'll be improving their communication skills, too!

Word Of The Day

Increase your students' vocabularies by spotlighting a different vocabulary word each day. Choose a word from the dictionary that is unfamiliar to your students and write it on the chalkboard. At the beginning of the day, have each child write on a small strip of paper what he thinks the word means. Ask students to place their strips in a designated container, such as a decorated coffee can. Whenever there is any extra time during the day, read some of the students' definitions aloud. Then at the end of the day, write the real definition of the word on the chalkboard. Discuss its meaning with the class and ask for volunteers to use the word in a sentence. By the end of the school year, your students will have quite an assortment of words in their spelling, listening, and reading vocabularies.

Ann Margaret Eddy—Gr. 2
Royal Oaks Christian School
Arroyo Grande, CA

I think voyage is a car.

Deanna

I think voyage is a boat.

Thomas

today we are, going on a field trip to the zoo?

Morning Eye-Opener

Energize your youngsters for a full day of learning with this wake-up call! Each morning write a sentence on the chalkboard that contains punctuation and grammar usage errors. (Famous quotations or special instructions the students will need for the day are good ideas for sentences.) Have students locate the errors in the sentence, then copy the sentence correctly on pieces of paper. Afterward enlist students' help in identifying the sentence's errors. As the year goes by, incorporate the spelling rule of the week, or ask students to add adjectives to the corrected sentence. Collect the papers and use them for a variety of purposes, such as evaluating your students' language abilities and monitoring handwriting neatness throughout the year. Students will definitely be wide awake after this daily morning activity.

Helen D. Gromadzki—Math Grs. 1–3
Bollman Bridge Elementary School
Jessup, MD

Dictionary Relay

Students will be off and running—their fingers through the dictionary with this group activity! Before playing the game, be sure to review the use of guide words with your students. To begin, write a list of vocabulary words on an overhead transparency and cover them with a sheet of paper. Provide a dictionary for each student. Uncover one word from the transparency and have students look up the word in their dictionaries. The first student to locate the word tells the others what page it is on and reads the definition. If desired, give that student a special treat. Continue the game by showing one vocabulary word at a time. By the end of the year, your students will have prizewinning dictionary skills! Ready, set, go!

Elaine Parr—Gr. 2
Copeland Elementary
Houston, TX

Around The World

Here's a one-of-a-kind way to help students review a variety of information. Have students sit in a large circle formation; then choose one student to stand behind the first contestant in the circle. Ask those two students a question relating to any subject area. If the person standing answers the question first, she moves clockwise around the circle to the next person sitting and the game continues. If the contestant sitting answers the question first, she changes places with the person standing and also moves clockwise around the circle to the next person sitting. The game continues until each child has had a chance to answer a question. Students will be thrilled at the chance to challenge a classmate!

Janet Lukacs—Reading Teacher
Blairsville Elementary
Blairsville, PA

Hook A Fish

Reel in your students for this review game that adds a fishing twist to the traditional game of hangman. The game can be used to review a variety of subjects, such as vocabulary or math facts. Divide the class into two teams. Draw two stringers on the chalkboard, as shown. Label each stringer with a different number. To begin play, the teacher asks a member from team one a question pertaining to the area that is being reviewed. If the team member answers the question correctly, his team receives a fish on one of the team's hooks. If the team member answers the question incorrectly, the other team has a chance to answer the question and receive a fish. The game continues until one team wins with a stringer full of fish. Ready to play? Then cast a line of questions to your youngsters!

Peter Tucciarone—Gr. 3
Rowan Elementary
Cranberry Township, PA

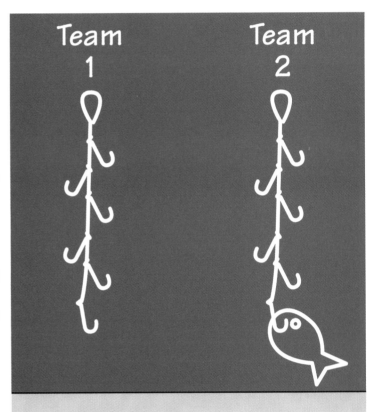

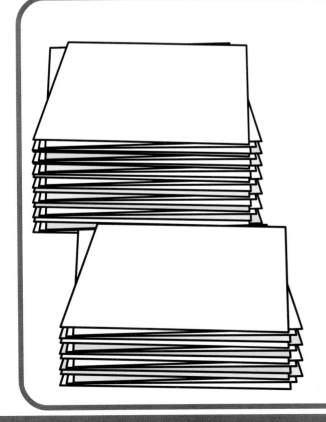

Paper Shortage

Add a twist to the daily routine and encourage paper conservation at the same time with a pretend paper shortage. The day before the paper shortage, collect and count all of the paper that your students used during the day. Record the number and set the stack aside in a box. On the morning of the paper shortage, ask each student to estimate how many sheets of paper she uses in a day. Record each student's response and calculate the total. Throughout the day, have each student complete all of her assignments using only one sheet of paper. At the end of the day, collect and stack students' papers. Compare this stack to the one in the box. In addition, share students' estimates of the number of sheets of paper usually used with the actual number used yesterday. Your youngsters will be amazed at the results and more than ready to recycle at school and home.

Storybook Character Party

It doesn't have to be Halloween for you and your students to dress up. Plan a storybook character party in your classroom! In the days prior to the party, ask your principal, assistant principal, librarian, and secretary to each choose a book and come dressed up as one of its characters. On the day of the party, invite each student to choose a favorite book and come to school dressed as one of the book's characters. (Be sure to dress as a storybook character yourself.) Have each child share details from his chosen story; then have him challenge his classmates to guess his identity. After everyone has shared his costume, celebrate with cookies and punch. What a fun way to get to know the characters in a variety of stories!

Susan Smith—Gr. 1
Canterbury Woods School, Fairfax, VA

Wanted:
Marvelous Memories!

Test your students' memories with this quiet, indoor game. Gather students in a circle and place a class supply of different objects, such as balls and bottles of glue, in the middle of the circle. Select a child to be It. It touches an object in the middle, then taps the child to his right on the shoulder. The second child touches the object It touched, touches an additional object, and then taps the child to his right. For as long as time permits, each remaining student takes a turn, adding an object to the series. During his turn, a student may tap another child if he needs help to remember the order in which the objects were touched. Be on the lookout for a class full of observant students!

Morning Question

A little bit of colored water and a few containers are all you need for a daily morning warm-up activity. Each morning set out three see-through one-liter containers and a large bowl of colored water with a small scoop. Write a question on the chalkboard that requires a choice of one of three answers, such as "What is your favorite place to swim?" Next label each of the three containers with one of the possible answers, such as "ocean," "pool," or "lake." As each student enters the classroom, he reads the question and takes one scoop of water from the bowl and pours it into the container that represents the answer he chose. After everyone has answered the question, ask students to look at the water levels to see which answer was the most popular. What a fun way to start the morning—wet and learning!

Debbie Cowden—Gr. 3
Hawley School
Newtown, CT

What is your favorite place to swim?

ocean | pool | lake

Food

The incredible, edible egg

Chicken

MILK

Cooperative Classification

Sharpen students' vocabulary and higher level thinking skills with this cooperative learning activity. Give each group of students a sheet of chart paper programmed with a category name such as *food, animals,* or *toys.* Then, working cooperatively, have each group search through newspapers and magazines to find words or pictures appropriate for its category. When a student locates a potential item, he shares it with his group. If his group agrees that it fits the category, the student cuts out the word or picture and glues it onto the chart paper. After a predetermined amount of time, invite a spokesperson from each group to share the items from their category. Classification and social skills will be on a steady incline after a few rounds of this cooperative lesson.

X Marks The Items

Here's an indoor activity that tests your students' luck and listening skills. Choose a category such as numbers, alphabet letters, foods, or names of classmates. Have each student write ten items from the category on his paper. After all students have finished their lists, call out items in the category at random. Students cross out any items on their lists that are called. The first child to mark out all the items on his paper is the winner.

Rapid Review

Add excitement to test reviews with this rapid review! Place a class supply of numbered skill cards in various spots around the classroom. Each student needs a sheet of paper and a pencil to begin. To begin, students each find a card and write the number and answer to the card. When a signal is given, they check their answers by turning over their skill cards. When the teacher gives the signal again, students take their pencils and papers and move to another spot in the room. Repeat this procedure until students have answered each skill card. This game can be used with a variety of skills such as addition facts, place value, and vocabulary words.

Have You Heard?

Wrap up your school year with this fact-based writing activity, and prepare the makings of a bulletin board for next year at the same time. Ask each student to draw a picture of himself, then write a noteworthy fact about you on writing paper (cut in the shape of a speech bubble). The fact should be something the student wants to share with children who will enter that classroom next year. When fall rolls around, post the pictures and student comments on a bulletin board titled "Have You Heard About [your name]?" This friendly way of introducing yourself will certainly be convincing to your new students since the comments come directly from former students.

Jan House—Gr. 3
Crabapple Crossing Elementary
Alpharetta, GA

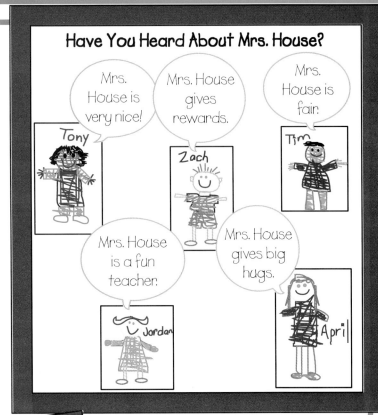

Have You Heard About Mrs. House?

Mrs. House is very nice!

Mrs. House gives rewards.

Mrs. House is fair.

Mrs. House is a fun teacher.

Mrs. House gives big hugs.

Classmate Crossword

Prepare this class-pleasing crossword puzzle to put the finishing touch on your school year. To create a crossword puzzle, design a puzzle grid so that each student's first name fits into the puzzle; then compose a crossword clue for each student in your class. Your students will enjoy reminiscing about the year and solving the clue that matches each class member.

Michelle Sharp—Grs. 1–3
Kathryn Winn Primary School
Carrollton, KY

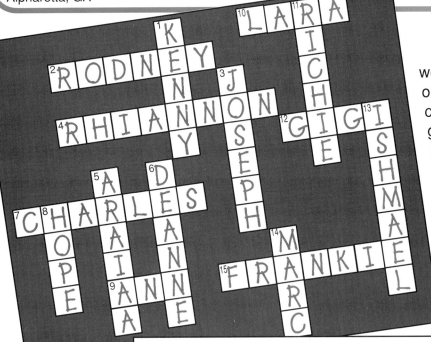

Across

2. He sang "The Star-Spangled Banner" for the class.
4. She's from Holland.
7. He plays the trumpet.
9. She likes animals.
10. She has red hair.
12. She is really good in Science.
15. He has twin sisters.

Down

1. He has two big dogs.
3. He has done a lot of plays.
5. She's a good dancer.
6. She is very quiet.
8. She rides her bike to school.
11. He is Italian.
13. He likes to tell stories.
14. He has a great smile.

Year's End Raffle

Clean out your closets and drawers to eliminate a multitude of items from years gone by. Round up an assortment of old books, puzzles, games, stuffed animals, pens, mugs, or toys that are no longer needed in your classroom. Plan a raffle at the end of the year to give each student an opportunity to take home one or more of these treasures—for keeps! Your students will be thrilled with an opportunity to own a cherished keepsake, while you will be pleased to have a tidy room and much needed space.

Liesl Collins—Gr. 3
Littleton Elementary School
Cashion, AZ

Review The Year From A To Z

As your school year nears its end, have students brainstorm their favorite events of the year using this unique approach. Divide your students into small groups. Ask each group to brainstorm and write one or more thoughts about their school year for each letter of the alphabet. The letter *A* might include: adding, alphabet, animals, astronauts, etc. Reward a prize to the group with the most ideas. Then separate your groups and assign each student a letter of the alphabet. Give each child the list of ideas collected for his letter and ask him to illustrate a page for a class alphabet book. The student-made page must contain the assigned letter, a picture of one item from the list, and a small caption explaining the picture. Assemble the pages in order to form an alphabet memory book to share with the whole class. Add to the life of the book by reading it on the first day of school the following year. It will give your new students an advanced look at the exciting year that awaits them.

Kristin Rowley—Gr. 2, Clara H. Carlson School, Elmont, NY

Tell It Like It Was

Give your outgoing students a writing task that will be a treat to future readers. Ask each of your students to compose a letter to a student who will enter their classroom next school year. Suggest that they tell the incoming students about their teacher, their classroom, and interesting events that took place during the year. At the start of the next school year, send each of your new students one of the letters written by a former student. The new students and their parents will look forward to an exciting year after reading the encouraging comments regarding their year ahead—as told by someone who's been there!

Leigh Anne Newsom
E. W. Chittum School
Chesapeake, VA

Dear Friend,

You will really love third grade! We learned how to write cursive. Mrs. Newsom likes to play fun games.

Your friend,
Mark

*Clue 1: Take down the writing bulletin board. Check with your teacher. Go to Bobby's desk for clue 2.

*Clue 2: Wash the art table. Check with your teacher. Go to pencil sharpener for clue 3.

Treasure Hunt Cleanup

Ahoy, Mateys! There's treasure to be found in this cleanup activity. Host a treasure hunt to clean up your classroom on the last day of school! Divide students into teams of three to four members each. Write clues that include cleanup chores on paper and hide them around the room. Make several clues for each group. Each clue should direct students to their next clue. With the last clue, direct students to a special treat for a job well done!

Summer Dos

Enlist your students' help to create a list of 100 things to do during summer vacation. Write student suggestions on chart paper as the class brainstorms; then type the list and duplicate student copies. Distribute the list on the last day of school as you send students off for an educational summer vacation.

87. Ride a bike.
88. Go fishing.
89. Watch a movie.
90. Catch a bug.
91. Wash a car.

Bring A Game

For a change of routine at the year's end, have each child bring a game to share with the class on a predetermined play day. Separate the students into small groups, and have each child in turn teach his game to his group. Not only is this fun for students, but it also reinforces the skills of giving and following directions. Be sure to bring a game yourself and join in the fun!

Susan

I liked the arts and crafts fair.

Charles

I liked going on our field trip to the farm.

Memory Books

Students are the authors of this end-of-the-year book. Have each child draw a self-portrait on a sheet of white paper and write his favorite memory of the school year. Duplicate enough copies of each memory for every student. Help each child staple his copies of the memories together to make a booklet. Then let your children have fun autographing their pictures in their classmates' booklets. The booklets will be great keepsakes of the past year.

Summer Review

Don't send your students home for the summer empty-handed. Prepare a summer workbook for each of your students. Include practice sheets in areas where improvement is needed. Also include fun pages featuring some of the students' favorite types of puzzles and activities. Surround each book's pages with a construction-paper cover, and staple the edge. Add a sticker and a title to each cover. Then surprise your students with this special treat on the last day of school. Both parents and students will appreciate your efforts!

Notes Of Appreciation

During the last week of school, ask each student to create a note of appreciation for each parent volunteer. It is a great way to end the school year on a positive note and gives students a lesson in consideration. When the notes are finished, invite the volunteers to the classroom for a party of appreciation. Serve cookies and punch as students deliver their thank-you notes. The good feelings will be shared all around.

Reading Day

During the last week of school, sponsor an all-day read-in in your classroom. Ask each student to bring several books (labeled with her name), a large comfortable pillow or sleeping bag, and a nutritious snack for the event. Begin the day with students reading their own books. After a set amount of time, ring a bell to signal students to switch books with their neighbors. Continue in this manner until students have had the chance to read a variety of books. Then have a read-aloud session with follow-up activities, and other organized reading events such as partner, small group, and choral readings. Students will enjoy the relaxing pace of the day and will get to show off the reading progress they've made throughout the year.

Any Beautiful Collectible
For The Classroom

Dear Parent,

In order to enhance our school year, I invite you to join in a scavenger hunt! If you can, please assist your child in bringing in your extra ABCs…Any Beautiful Collectibles for the classroom.

A: art supplies, aluminum pie pans
B: baskets, balloons, buttons
C: clothespins, cotton balls, crayons, craft sticks
D: dried lima beans, dominos
E: erasers, envelopes
F: felt, film canisters (from 35mm film rolls), folders
G: glue
H: hangers
I: index cards
J: jars with lids
K: Kleenex®
L: liquid soap, lunch bags
M: magazines, magnets, markers
N: notebooks, napkins
O: old books for the reading corner
P: paper clips, paper, pencils, paper plates, pipe cleaners
Q: quick and easy ideas you wish to share
R: ribbons, rubber bands
S: seasonal items, stickers, sponges, straws
T: tissue paper, tape, treats
U: uncooked macaroni
V: volunteers in the classroom
W: writing supplies, warm smiles
X: Xerox® paper
Y: yarn
Z: Ziploc® bags

Thank you!

_____
(teacher's name)

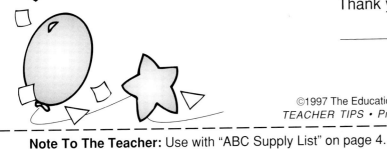

Note To The Teacher: Use with "ABC Supply List" on page 4.

Pattern

Use with "Whoo Am I?" on page 13.

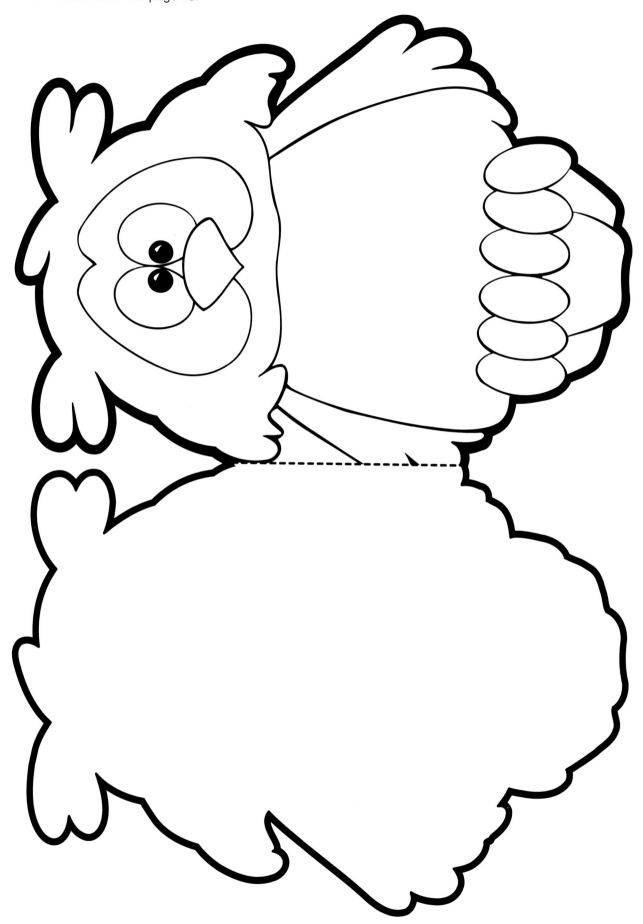

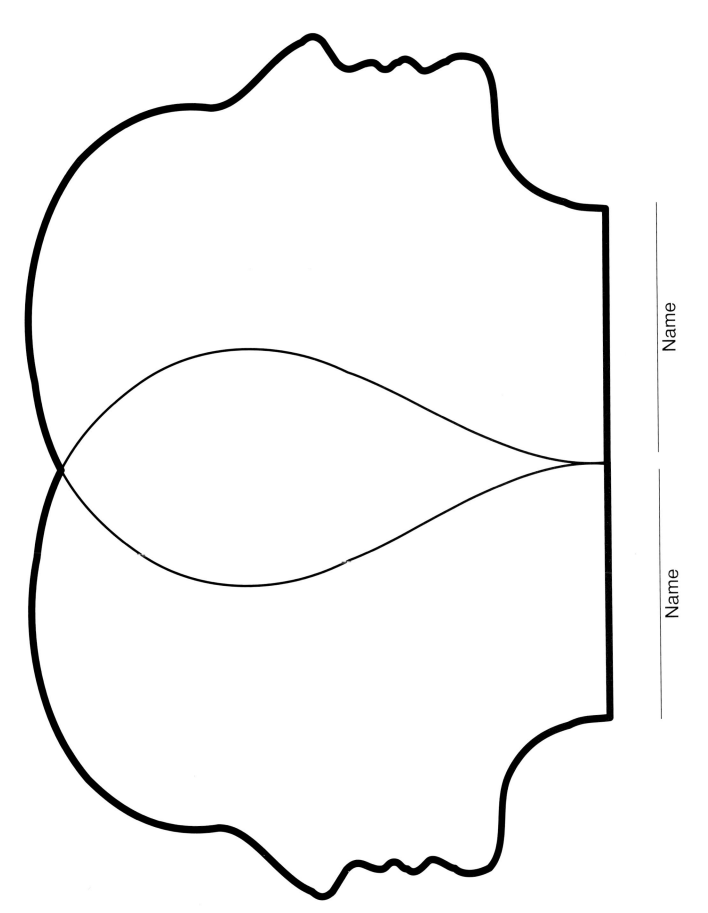

Name

Name

_____ 's
(name)

Favorite Things

Color	Sport
Season	**Book**
Subject	**Food**
TV show	**Animal**

Note To The Teacher: Use with "Star Of The Week" on page 22.

Name: _____   Date: _____

Problem Report

Draw or write your answers.

What happened?	Why did it happen?

How do you feel?

How do you think the other person feels?

If this happens again, what could you do to solve the problem?

Signed: _____

(student)

_____

(teacher)

Consequence determined by teacher: _____

Note To The Teacher: Use with "Problem Report" on page 38.

Pattern
Use with "Welcoming A New Bunch Of Students!" on page 65.

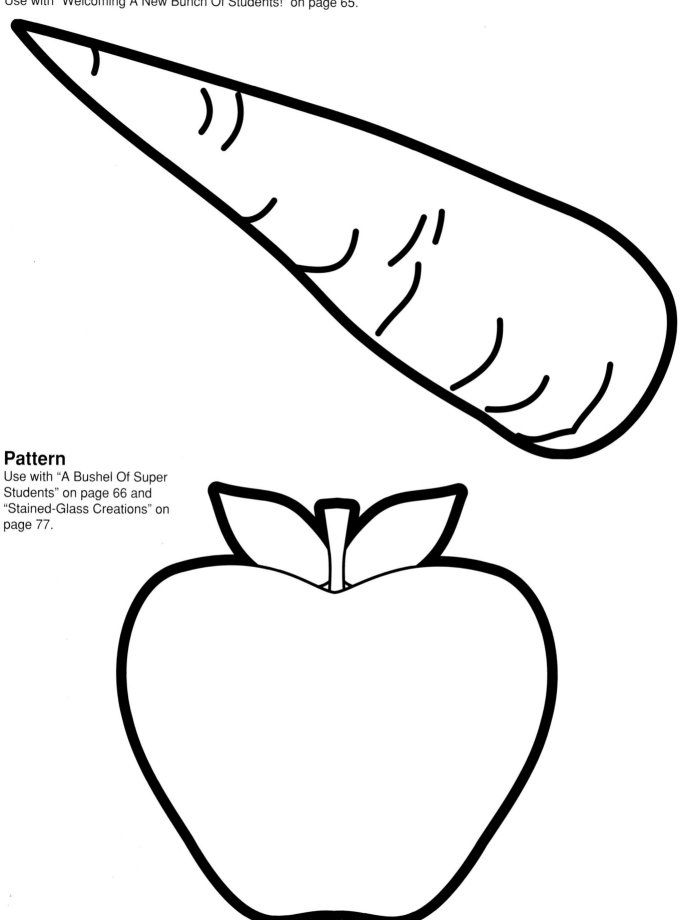

Pattern
Use with "A Bushel Of Super Students" on page 66 and "Stained-Glass Creations" on page 77.

Pattern

Use with "Let's Explore A New Grade!" on page 67.

Pattern

Use with "Million-Dollar Students" on page 70.

Pattern
Use with "Jammin' Jobs" on page 69.

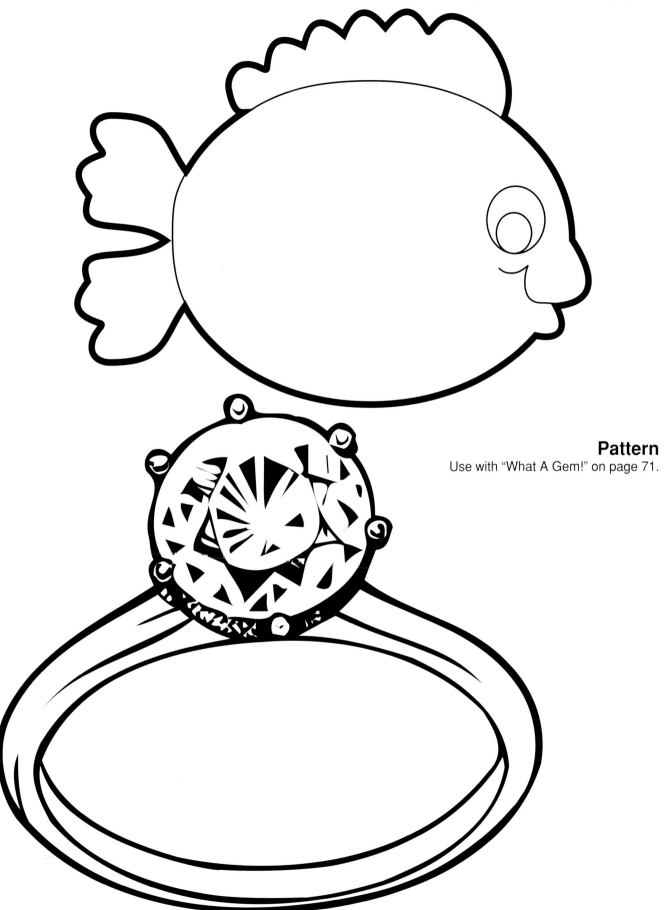

Pattern
Use with "We're Swimming Towards Success!" on page 69.

Pattern
Use with "What A Gem!" on page 71.

Patterns
Use with "We Go Bananas Over Books" on page 70.

Pattern

Use with "Recycled Spelling" on page 103.

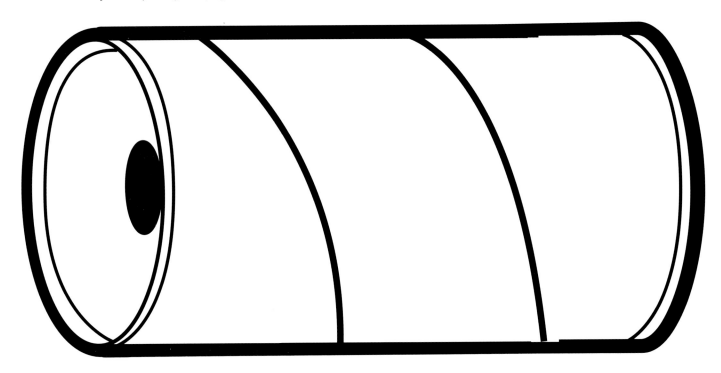

Pattern

Use with "Telephone Spelling" on page 104.

1	2 ABC	3 DEF
4 GHI	5 JKL	6 MNO
7 PRS	8 TUV	9 WXY
	0 QZ	

1	2 ABC	3 DEF
4 GHI	5 JKL	6 MNO
7 PRS	8 TUV	9 WXY
	0 QZ	

State Search

The state of the week is_____.

Find the state on the map below and color it red.

What is the capital of this state?_____

Draw and color the state flag.

Draw and color the state bird.